ABOUT OMEGA

Omega was founded in 1977 at a time when holistic health, psychological inquiry, world music and art, meditation, and new forms of spiritual practice were just budding in American culture. Omega was then just a small band of seekers searching for new answers to perennial questions about human health and happiness. The mission was as simple as it was large: to look everywhere for the most effective strategies and inspiring traditions that might help people bring more meaning and vitality into their lives.

Since then, Omega has become the nation's largest holistic learning center. Every year more than 25,000 people attend workshops, retreats, and conferences in health, psychology, the arts, and spirituality on its eighty-acre campus in the countryside of Rhinebeck, New York, and at other sites around the country. While Omega has grown in size, its mission remains the same. Omega is not aligned with any particular healing method or spiritual tradition. Its programs feature all of the world's wisdom traditions and are committed to offering people an opportunity to explore their own path to better health, personal growth, and inner peace.

The name Omega was inspired by the writings of Pierre Teilhard de Chardin, a twentieth-century mystic and philosopher who used the word to describe the point within each one of us where our inner spiritual nature meets our outer worldly nature. Teilhard believed that the synthesis of these two domains presented the greatest challenge—and the greatest hope—for human evolution. Of his belief in the balance between world and spirit, Teilhard wrote, "I am going to broadcast the seed and let the wind carry it where it will."

Omega has taken on the task of helping spread that seed so that a better world for all of us can continue to take root and grow.

OMEGA
Institute for Holistic Studies

40

The Omega Institute
Mind, Body, Spirit Series

An Omega Institute Mind, Body, Spirit Book

Bodywork Basics

A GUIDE TO THE

POWERS AND PLEASURES

OF YOUR BODY

Anne Kent Rush

A DELL TRADE PAPERBACK

A DELL TRADE PAPERBACK

Published by
Dell Publishing
a division of
Random House, Inc.
1540 Broadway
New York, New York 10036

Written by: Anne Kent Rush
Series Consulting Editor: Robert Welsch
Series Editor: Kathleen Jayes
Series Manager: James Kullander
Literary Representative: Ling Lucas, Nine Muses and Apollo Inc.
Illustrations by: Howard R. Roberts (HROBERTSD@aol.com)

Cover photo copyright © 2000 by Mel Yates/FPG International
(Top row and bottom left); Justin Pumfrey/FPG International
(Bottom right)
Cover design by Royce Becker

Dell books may be purchased for business or promotional use or for special sales.
For information please write to: Special Markets Department,
Random House, Inc., 1540 Broadway, New York, N.Y. 10036.

DTP and the colophon are trademarks of Random House, Inc.

Library of Congress Cataloging-in-Publication Data
Rush, Anne Kent
    Bodywork basics : a guide to the powers and pleasures of your
body /by Anne Kent Rush
        p.   cm.—(The Omega Institute mind, body, spirit series)
    ISBN 0-440-50870-3
    1. Holistic medicine.   2. Alternative medicine.   3. Mind
and body—Health aspects.   4. Self-care. Health.   I. Title.
    II. Series.
    R733.Z45 2000
    615.5—dc21   99-36563
                                                        CIP

Printed in the United States of America

Published simultaneously in Canada

January 2000

10 9 8 7 6 5 4 3 2 1

RRD

BOOK DESIGN BY JENNIFER ANN DADDIO

Omega Institute sends out heartfelt thanks and appreciation
to staff members and teachers for their support
and contribution in the preparation
and publishing of this book.

Note to the Reader

Contents

Bodywork

Basics

One

❖

Invitation

to

Exploration

Introduction to Bodywork

What Is Bodywork?

Bodywork includes a variety of physical and mental exercises aimed at increasing your self-awareness and communication, through broadening your experience of all your senses. Bodywork emphasizes your involvement in your own healing and in learning about your body. The techniques described in this book are listed in alphabetical order for simple access. Most major Bodywork systems are included, but there are too many for every one to be covered here. Hopefully the basic systems described in this book will supply the groundwork for understanding any of the varieties you may encounter. The techniques are divided into three categories based on their origin: Western, Eastern, and East/West combined.

Health is wholeness and balance, an inner resilience that allows you to meet the
demands of living without being overwhelmed, [and thus] brings with
it a sense of strength and joy.

—ANDREW WEIL, M.D.,

How Is It Different from Medicine?

Western medicine as it is practiced today is based on the premise that your bodily problems are cured by external means (setting bones, adjusting posture, having surgery) and by prescribing drugs to be taken. Bodywork focuses on learning exercises to trigger your internal healing processes, and on increasing body awareness. Bodywork is the basis for much of the preventive health-care and alternative health-care techniques now being introduced to complement traditional Western medicine.

Who Does What Where?

Usually you can schedule Bodywork treatments at a health spa, sports club, wellness centers, and from private therapists. Each system features self-care as well as therapist-administered treatments. To practice as a Bodywork therapist you would need to train for certification in the technique of your choice. To begin your personal exploration, simple techniques you can practice on yourself and with others, without special training, are described in this book. When you try them, you can sample the systems and experience the basics of each Bodywork.

Invitation to Exploration

Inviting someone into the world of Bodywork is like introducing him or her to a wonderful new friend. The process of getting to know someone is exciting and full of mystery and surprises. Friendship takes time and effort to blossom. Exploring Bodywork demands a measure of attention and commitment on your part, because you will be taking in a great deal of information. Luckily the learning comes mainly through pleasure, growth, and play. Bodywork is the doorway to explore the lands and language of your body. And these endlessly exotic realms are right under your nose.

You have a lot to gain from getting to know Bodywork. Like a really good friend Bodywork will be there for you when the chips are down. You'll learn powerful new techniques for reducing stress, relieving pain, and healing emotional and physical wounds.

Bodywork is also there when things are going well, and you're ready to celebrate. Bodywork can heighten your joys, increase your pleasures, improve your health, and broaden the treasures you can offer others through sharing these fun techniques.

Many of the originators of the different schools of Bodywork are as interesting as their systems. The tales of how techniques evolved can be fascinating. Their stories of triumph over adversity are inspiring. Each unique system bears the mark of the personality of its inventor. Besides investigating the basics of the techniques and their effects, learning about some of the qualities of the founders can help you match up your preferred tastes and temperament with a compatible system.

Of course, as Joe E. Brown wisely remarks to Jack Lemmon at the conclusion of the film *Some Like It Hot,* "Nobody's perfect." Certain Bodywork techniques or therapists may not be right for you. So apply the same commonsense guidelines to experimenting with Bodywork that you would when making a new acquaintance. Don't let someone into your home and heart until you've checked her out well. Get references for practitioners from respected professionals. Trust your own gut reactions to a technique. When you start your exploration, you may not know much about the details of a system, but you will always know whether it feels right for you or not. When you have done your homework and are satisfied in your choices, relax and enjoy yourself. Be ready for layer after layer of interesting revelation, challenge, pleasure, and triumph. Remember, good friendships grow better the longer you're involved in them.

As always, the greatest gifts of friendship come through sharing more of yourself at your most generous, due to your expanded sense of balance and self-enrichment. Your best new friend from exploring Bodywork will be a healthier, more alive, more joyous you. We are all on a journey of learning and exploration. So come join us. We're looking forward to meeting you!

A Family History of Bodywork

Who Is the Mother of Bodywork?

Modern Bodywork has a mother. Her name is Elsa Gindler. She lived and worked in Germany but before she died in 1961, she trained the key teachers of Bodywork who would come to the United States and introduce the work in America. All the original body systems in the Human Potential Movement are either descendants of Elsa Gindler's system *Arbeit am Menschen,* or Working with Human Beings, which brought mind and body work together, or of psychiatrist Wilhelm Reich's Orgone Therapy.

In Berlin, in her twenties, Gindler contracted tuberculosis. The only treatments

There is no genius whose followers have not improved on him.

—MOSHE FELDENKRAIS, D.SC.

known then, in the early years of the century, were rest and fresh air. Her doctors prescribed residence in a sanitorium in the Alps. She was told the alternative was death.

Unable to afford the expensive sanitoriums, Gindler determined to develop her own treatment. Her plan was to teach herself to breathe with her one healthy lung in order to allow the tuberculosis-infected lung to recuperate. She could find no such programs in books, so she worked for a year developing and using her own breathing awareness program. Her doctor's prediction that Gindler would die within a month proved inaccurate. She lived to the age of seventy-six.

She expanded her breathing program to include movement exercises and emotional work. Basing her thinking on philosophies of the ancient Egyptians and Greeks, Gindler developed techniques for uniting body and mind in new, gentle ways. She decided to teach her methods to others.

Where Did Bodywork Begin?

Living in Berlin during World War II, Gindler continued her exercise classes. She gave stress-reduction training to enable her clients to cope with the difficulties of hiding in air raid shelters. Opposed to the Nazis, she sheltered Jews. She escaped being sent to a concentration camp herself, but after a Jewish family whom Gindler hid in her home was discovered and killed, and Gindler's home fire-bombed by Nazi youth, she developed an intestinal ulcer and also suffered from malnutrition from lack of food.

Despite her frail health Gindler lived many more years and trained practitioners, including Magdalene Proskauer and Charlotte Selver, in her groundbreaking system. Magda Proskauer came to New York to work with lung patients in hospitals before she moved to San Francisco and started a private practice. Her Proskauer Awareness technique, developed from Gindler's work, became one of the cornerstones of early Bodywork development in the U.S. Charlotte Selver also moved to the U.S. and taught her Sensory Awareness system at Esalen Institute and elsewhere. Sensory Awareness brought Zen philosophy together with body awareness and was one of the most important foundations of Bodywork.

Who Is the Father of Bodywork?

Bodywork has two fathers, one Austrian, one Chinese. Austrian Wilhelm Reich, a psychiatrist (1897–1957), noticed that his patients' emotional problems had corresponding physical expressions. Reich developed exercises for his patients to help release the physical tension related to their emotional conflicts. When Dr. Reich used both body and mind work with his patients, they progressed much more quickly than with talking alone.

Reich left Europe during World War II to escape political persecution. He moved to the U.S. and practiced as a psychiatrist, including his body techniques in his work. A few foresighted therapists recognized Reich's genius and trained with him. But unfortunately the therapeutic climate in the United States in the 1950s was not advanced enough for Reich's radical work. He was harassed and put in jail for practicing unorthodox methods. He did not live to see his work become the foundation of Bioenergetics therapy and of many of the techniques of Bodywork that we know today.

From Europe, Doris Breyer was a German student of Reich, who moved to San Francisco to establish her Bodywork practice. She strongly influenced many Bodywork practitioners in the 1970s and helped Reich's ideas to flourish. Breyer and Proskauer were close colleagues.

The Eastern father of modern Bodywork is Huang Ti, the Yellow Emperor. He lived from 2697 to 2596 B.C. and is thought to have been the first ruler to organize and record the powerful healing traditions of ancient China. Between 100 and 300 B.C. his records were compiled into one book, the *Nei Ching*, the Yellow Emperor's

Classic of Internal Medicine. The *Nei Ching* showed the influence of the philosopher Lao Tzu (born about 600 B.C.), who developed the school of thought known as Taoism. Characterized by the belief that change is reality, Taoist principles are reflected in Acupuncture. The *Nei Ching* is the constant foundation of Eastern Bodywork. All the modern Bodywork systems that we know now owe their birth and development to the work of the brilliant original pioneers described in this chapter.

What Is the Difference Between Bodywork and Body Therapy?

This book includes many varieties of Bodywork. Several closely related techniques exist that have been excluded because they fall into the category of Body Therapy. The difference is one of emphasis. Body Therapy emphasizes deep emotional exploration through verbal psychological therapy, using body techniques as supplements to inten-

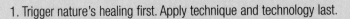

Six Tenets of Alternative Medicine

1. Trigger nature's healing first. Apply technique and technology last.

2. Practice patient-centered rather than physician-centered care.

3. Do no harm.

4. Generally expect results to take longer.

5. Prescribe natural, whole substances.

6. Base goals on higher definitions of good health.

—Dr. Bernie Siegel

sify the emotional work. Bodywork emphasizes body exploration, with the emotional connections acknowledged but not pursued in deep therapy.

Body Therapy requires a longtime commitment from the client, and the techniques are not safe for an untrained person to do. In contrast Bodywork can be enjoyed either on a short-term basis simply for relaxation and posture realignment, or used long-term for stress management. Bodywork requires less training than Body Therapy and is safe and pleasant for most people to do. Bodywork gives you a chance to make good health fun.

Exploring the Powers and Pleasures of Your Body

Learning Bodywork

Every culture adopts an attitude about how to approach the body. Western medicine traditionally separates healing your body from healing your mind. Bodywork brings the two together. Bodywork treatments combine physical and psychological healing and aim at making them accessible to the average person in simple ways in daily life.

There are so many different types of Bodywork techniques that you are bound to find one that matches your personal tastes. There are speedy, high-energy, demanding, sometimes painful healing techniques. There are slow-paced, gentle, noninvasive pleasure-based healing techniques. And there is every combination of these extremes in between.

No one can tell you exactly which Bodywork system is best for you. When you learn some basics and test a few, you can choose the one or more that suit your needs and personality. Trying out varieties of Bodywork in your search for your staple favorites is half the fun of the journey. More than likely when you finally think you have your mind made up and your routine set, someone will invent a new system, and there will be more pleasures to test.

Why Am I Doing This?

You may begin your exploration of Bodywork to soothe a specific ache, pain, or a psychological conflict. You may also explore out of a desire to expand your physical horizons and become a more sensual person. All of these approaches are valid. Your goals will change with your needs.

Stress-reduction techniques can improve your responses to crisis. Postural-alignment techniques can help you feel more comfortable as you move through your daily routines, as well as improve performance during sports. Mind/Body techniques can deepen your emotional relationships. Sensory-Awareness techniques can expand your realm of pleasures. All Bodywork can improve your general health so that you are better able to cope with crisis and to maintain your body's balance.

Bodywork systems are the basis for much of what is becoming known as preventive health care today. Bodywork techniques can be used as therapy in case of illness or injury. But the major focus of Bodywork is to improve the quality of your everyday life.

The information offered here is a sampling of the cornucopia of Bodywork options. By trying the exercises you can taste-test a technique, but the satisfaction of a full meal comes with a complete treatment or more specialized training. Hopefully these basic exercises will inspire you to make Bodywork a basic resource and pleasure in your life.

To Receive

Receiving is an art in itself. It's possible to have a Bodywork session and miss a lot of the relaxation and pleasure if you are uncomfortable or nervous. Some simple preparation should increase your enjoyment and turn you into an expert in the art of receiving the most pleasure from your Bodywork.

- **Gather information** on the techniques and the practitioner beforehand. First read about the Bodywork to familiarize yourself with the process. Then you can select the most appropriate one for your condition and ease any nervousness from unfamiliarity. Second, unscrupulous or badly trained practitioners can be avoided if you do your homework. A referral from a trusted friend, a doctor, or a professional organization specializing in your specific technique is important. Organizations that train and award credentials to practitioners can be contacted for referrals to a reliable therapist.

- **Remember you're the boss.** Even though you may not be an expert in the Bodywork technique, you are an expert in yourself. You know what feels good or not. Don't be shy about expressing your preference. You also always have the choice to remain partially or fully clothed if you prefer. You're paying for this. This is your treat to yourself to help you relax and feel better. You set the terms. Never allow anyone to do something you don't like on the excuse "That's the way it's done." Tell him to stop or to do it differently.

- **Be communicative** when necessary. Before the treatment, let the practitioner know what your interests are and what you expect. Talk over any questions you have. During the treatment be specific if you would like the practitioner to either stop or change what he is doing. If the therapist is pressing too hard, you can simply say, "Much lighter pressure, please," Or say, "Deeper pressure, please," if the massage is too light. Be sure to explain if you have any sore or injured areas that should be avoided. Let your therapist know if you want to focus on one or two areas rather than the whole body.

- **Use your breathing to deepen your relaxation.** If you breathe high in your chest, this keeps you alert and awake. The deeper you breathe in your body, the more relaxed you will become. Allow your whole chest and abdomen to rise slightly as you inhale, and then sink down a bit as you exhale. The more you involve your abdominal muscles in the deep breaths, the more peaceful you will feel. Slow down the pace of your breathing. Instead of short high breaths, take long, deep ones. You can use visualization to increase this relaxation. Imagine you can send your exhalation down through the center of your body and into your abdomen, legs, and even feet. Imagine you are sending warmth and circulation through your body with your breathing.

- **Talk as little as possible.** Bodywork focuses on the body's messages. This is primarily a nonverbal experience. To deepen the relaxation, focus on the sensations of touch and your responses. This is a vacation from talking. Enjoy your chance to forget the static of the outside world and to explore the inner world of your own thoughts and sensations. On the other hand, if you wish to explore your emotional responses to the physical work, discuss this with the therapist before the treatment so that the two of you agree on the role talking will play in your session.

- **Allow yourself some quiet, still time** at the close of the massage. Don't jump up right away. Rest with your eyes closed and do a mental inventory of how your body is feeling. Enjoy the relaxation and let it spread. Then sit up slowly and move into the rest of your day gradually. Ideally you'll have scheduled an hour or two of free time after your Bodywork session to enjoy your relaxed state. Or you can set your appointment for the end of the day so that you can surrender to the relaxation all evening.

To Give

Is giving really better than receiving? Recent studies show that giving massages lowers stress levels in your body and calms the giver to a measurable physiological degree. Learning to give Bodywork as well as to receive it can be deeply relaxing and rewarding. Several hints can help the giver stay as comfortable as the receiver.

- **Set the scene.** Arrange a room for the comfort of both the giver and receiver. Choose a quiet, warm, dimly lit place. If you are giving the massage, be sure the height of the table or bed is comfortable for you. You wouldn't want to throw your back out while relaxing someone else's. Remove watches and jewelry that might scratch. Check your hands. Be sure your fingernails are very short, and your hands are clean and oiled.

  Cover the massage table or bed with clean sheets or beach towels. Have enough extras on hand to fully cover the person in case she is chilly or very modest. And she'll need a clean towel to wipe off excess oil at the end of the massage. A vase of flowers or a potted plant adds a touch of natural luxury to the room.

+ **Have the oil ready** in two squeeze-top bottles so that one can be placed at the head and the other at the feet for easy access. Be sure the oil is room temperature or a bit warmer before you apply it. Any pure vegetable oil bought at a health-food store or grocery is good for your skin. Mineral oil is less beneficial to your skin than vegetable oil. Almond and safflower oils are especially smooth without being too sticky. They also have no strong scent of their own. Many people prefer an unscented massage oil. For fun, or for aromatherapy, you can add several drops of an essential oil such as mint, sandalwood, or almond. You can buy them at most bath supply shops and health-food stores. If the person you are massaging does not want oil, place a light cotton sheet over her and use it as a friction barrier as you rub or press.

+ **Ask what your friend or client wants.** Before the massage or treatment, briefly explain what is involved and invite the receiver to make her preferences clear. Giving a good massage involves enjoying someone else's pleasure. Always respect her wishes. You are offering a gift of relaxation and caring for her benefit. It is her choice to be nude or clothed, to have deep pressure or light, to have music or silence, to have a full-body treatment or one-area focus. Then encourage her to speak up during the massage if she wishes any changes. Ask about bruises, injuries, or tickle spots. These areas should be avoided.

+ **Relax.** If you are tense, the receiver will sense this, and the massage will be less comfortable for both of you. Before you begin, do some gentle deep breathing. Tune in to your body and notice where you feel tense. Make some light movements in the area to help release the tension. Mentally relax yourself also. Put cares and distractions from the rest of your day out of your mind and focus on the massage. This process will help relax both of you.

Your Hands

All Bodywork focuses largely on relaxing a person by touch. Your main instrument is your pair of hands. Hands are sensitive Bodywork tools with many nerves running to the spinal cord, which transmits messages to the brain. A single finger contains three thousand touch receptor nerve endings.

If you are receiving the Bodywork you will become very sensitive to the practitioner's hands and how they feel on your body. If you are giving, you will gradually develop a heightened awareness in your hands. When you begin learning to do Bodywork, it's wise to ask for regular verbal feedback. As you become more skilled and comfortable, the information you need will be transmitted through sensations in your hands.

Handy Tips for the Beginner

+ **Relax your hands.** Apply pressure by leaning your body weight into your arms and hands, rather than by pushing with your arm muscles. This will spare your arm and hand muscles much strain and allow you to achieve strong pressure. You won't tire as easily. This will feel more relaxing to the receiver also.

+ **Synchronize your movement with your breathing.** Imagine you can send your exhalation down your arms and into your hands to relax and warm them. Generally as you lean down and press, you exhale; as you lean back to release pressure, you inhale. Don't hold your breath. This will make you tense and slow down the flow of oxygen to your arms. Notice the breathing of the person you're massaging and try to synchronize your breathing with his.

+ **If you lose touch** with the person you're massaging, he will feel temporarily abandoned from care. A subtle way to deepen the comfort of your treatment is to keep one hand always touching the receiver.

+ **Move smoothly and rhythmically.** Timing is important for a relaxing treatment. Random stroking is disconcerting. Start slowly and work up to faster strokes. Then slow down as you conclude. Some people like to keep rhythm with music. Be sure to ask the receiver if he likes your selection.

- how to keep from tiring your hands
- how to relax the rest of your body while working hard with your hands
- how to increase the electromagnetic energy flow to your hands and into the other person to increase relaxation and healing
- how to sense with your hands where a person needs work
- how hard or softly to press
- how to feel when to avoid an area and when to linger

The Tickles

Everyone is a little ticklish on some spot of his body. The location of this spot is often a well-guarded secret. Before giving a massage it's a good idea to ask, "Is there anywhere you are sore or ticklish that I should avoid massaging?" Reassure him that you will stay away from these areas. Or with his permission you can try out some solutions. If the person is just slightly ticklish, massage oil can solve the problem

The Tickle Addict

Tickle addicts are mavericks: they love tickling more than any other skin contact. Light, feathery strokes send them into an alpha state. Stroking—without oils or any lubricant, directly on the skin—that would drive most others to reveal all their family secrets sends addicts into calm, endorphic rapture. For the most appreciated results, use your fingernails or fingertips to make repetitive, sweeping patterns on your friend's back. To present the tickle addict with a very special treat, give him or her a back rub or full body massage with feathers.

—Anne Kent Rush
The Back Rub Book:
How to Give and Receive Great Back Rubs; Vintage Books

because it eliminates the skin friction. Also, deepening your pressure helps because light touch is usually what triggers tickles. For this reason pressure-point techniques rather than long, smooth strokes are preferred by highly ticklish folks. Ticklish people may gravitate toward Acupressure, Polarity, and Shiatsu. Remaining fully clothed is an option for the extremely ticklish.

Emotions: Theirs

Most of the time Bodywork is a nonverbal experience. The major purpose of Bodywork is to explore the language and experience of the body, but from time to time talking becomes a natural part of this experience. During a treatment emotional reactions are normal. Most feelings will be those of pleasure, release, and relaxation. Along with the release of physical tension may come emotional reactions of sadness or anger connected to the cause of the tension. Don't be surprised to see a few tears or hear a few sighs. Some people like to note these reactions to themselves and resolve to clear up the causes at a later time. Other people may want to talk about what they are feeling during the treatment. Most often these are brief comments and serve to ease their tension. If there is an intense reaction, you may want to stop the massage to talk awhile.

If you are giving a massage to a friend or family member, you'll probably be comfortable enough together to talk the emotions over easily. You also won't be doing any complicated or deep enough therapy that you'd be likely to elicit traumatic emotional responses. Most of the time you'll just be hearing sounds of relaxation and pleasure. Only if you train to become a professional Body Therapist and practice deep-tissue release techniques as well as intense psychological work will you be likely to be faced with a client's traumatic emotional release. Always have a backup therapist's number on hand so that you can call for help if you feel out of your league. But for the beginner and layperson most emotional responses require common sense, sympathy, and brief reassurance.

Emotions: Yours

While giving a Bodywork treatment you may have emotional reactions that surprise you. You may feel sad while taking care of someone because you realize you need more care. Massaging one area, a foot or a hand for example, may trigger a memory of an old injury or an old pleasure that you had forgotten. The focus of the treatment should be the relaxation of the receiver. Your emotions should be mentally noted and dealt with later on your own. But remember that the power of Bodywork works both ways. Be on the alert for your personal reactions. This way you can keep them from interfering with the treatment. And you can benefit from the insight later.

Altered States

Most of us explore Bodywork both to relieve physical aches and pains and also to expand our sensory horizons. Bodywork can broaden our awareness of our own bodies as well as heighten our sensitivity to others'. During a Bodywork session you are more focused on your physical reactions than you would be at most other times, except perhaps during intense athletics or lovemaking. You will probably notice all sorts of sensations that you've had before but not brought to the forefront of your attention.

+ **During Bodywork you will probably notice for the first time many of the little physical tensions that can snowball into big pains.** Each of us has habitual unconscious stress responses. For example, if you tend to tighten your shoulders in response to anxiety, you might have a history of headaches or shoulder pains that you never understood came from this habit until something triggered it during a Bodywork session and the habit became conscious. Once you know where and how your pains begin, you can start changing your habits. For example, you can relax and lower your shoulders each time you feel them inching toward your ears. This new relaxation response can prevent a lot of future headaches.

+ **You'll probably discover some new areas of body pleasure during a session.** For instance, most people find hand massage deeply relaxing. The hand is an area many of us ignore when relaxing our bodies, but hands are areas of high stress. Since there are over three thousand nerve touch receptors in one finger alone, hand massage can have a profound tension-releasing effect. Massage on certain body areas will make you drowsy and on others will awaken you. These are practical points to know about yourself if you are having trouble sleeping or staying awake.

+ **You may become aware of your body's electric currents during a Bodywork session.** Your body's electromagnetic activity will be intensified during a good Bodywork session, especially if you are receiving Acupressure or Polarity Massage. We all have these currents operating throughout our bodies at all times, but relaxation and good Bodywork can intensify the flow of our electric energy. You will feel a slight tingling along your limbs when the energy flow is strengthened by the treatment. This is very good for your health. Some medical doctors apply electrostim machine treatments as part of a patient's physical therapy after an accident or injury to speed recovery. You can trigger the same energy release naturally through massage and other Bodywork to bolster your body's healing responses. Most people find the tingling sensation quite relaxing and pleasant.

+ **Toward the end of a terrific Bodywork session you may have the sensation that you are floating.** To most people this is a very pleasant feeling, although it makes some people nervous at first. It is a response to deep physical relaxation. When your muscles are contracted and tense, you feel as though you are weighted down. Your muscles are acting the way they do when you are carrying something heavy. When you release your muscle tension as a result of a relaxing massage, you feel as though a weight has been lifted. You feel lighter, almost as though you were floating. It's a wonderful vacation for your whole body to be relieved of the stress-induced tension. Your system needs periodic rests to renew. Enjoy this state.

Two

❖

Western

Bodywork

Introduction

What Is Western Bodywork?

Western Bodywork is made up of a variety of body-awareness techniques that are based on the premise that, to heal your body's illnesses and correct its imbalances, full, comfortable movement of the limbs is necessary.

How Is It Different from Eastern Bodywork?

While Western Bodywork focuses on postural alignment for movement comfort, Eastern Bodywork focuses on balancing our life energy. Eastern theories of body health center around belief in the healing powers of your body's electromagnetic energy currents. When these currents flow well, the body's systems all work.

> To find health should be the object of the doctor. Anyone can find disease.
>
> —DR. ANDREW TAYLOR STILL, FOUNDER OF OSTEOPATHIC MEDICINE

Who Does What Where?

Western Bodywork usually is available in wellness centers, health spas, sports clubs, and private practices of certified therapists. Training to become a Bodywork Therapist takes anywhere from six months to two years. Most techniques have professional organizations that offer therapist recommendations. Also you can practice many of the simple techniques on yourself or on others to sample the basics.

3.

The Alexander Technique

What and When

Alexander Technique is a system of gentle movements designed to align your posture and expand your range of motion. It aims to improve your quality of movement in dance and sports and can be used as a gentle physical therapy after injury. During a session you are usually fully clothed and moving according to instructions from the Alexander practitioner. Alexander is best learned from a teacher, due to the subtlety and spontaneity of the techniques.

Less Is More

If a Shaker craftsman invented a Bodywork system, it would be F. Matthias Alexander's technique . . . spare, eloquent, practical. Alexander believed that relaxed economy of movement would align your posture and relieve pain and stress. He developed a system of gentle movements that can erase bad postural habits and create comfortable, efficient physical performance.

Alexander was not a Shaker, but a Shakesperean actor from Tasmania who was plagued by the periodic loss of his voice while onstage. When no medical help cured the problem, Alexander took to examining himself in front of the mirror when in distress. He noted recurring postures accompanying the lost voice and developed his own movement sequences to relieve the problem. Alexander went on to develop a system for others to reeducate the body to maintain good movement patterns and thus to heal itself.

Think Tall

Alexander believed that when the head, neck, and torso are properly aligned, the spine lengthens and the head and neck rise to allow free, easy movement of the whole body. An Alexander teacher combines movement instruction with verbal guidance. Alexander recognized that physical instruction required mental participation by the client to take root and effect change.

The Alexander Technique is subtle, gentle, and exacting. It requires concentration and interest in detail. Because its goal is the complete reeducation of the way we use our bodies, it can be a long process made up of layers of physical and mental revelations. Alexander believed that ease of mind requires ease of movement.

If You Enroll in an Alexander Course

- ✦ Wear comfortable, loose clothes so you can move freely during the session.

- ✦ The teacher will instruct you in ways to improve your movement and to train your body to let go of tension-producing habits.

- ✦ The method is especially popular with dancers, actors, and athletes to improve performance. It is also particularly helpful to persons with serious spinal injuries, arthritis, and emphysema.

- ✦ An initial series of about thirty lessons is followed by a lapse in lessons so that your body can integrate the changes. Then periodic lessons can be taken to check and refresh your habits. Each series is tailored to the individual.

- ✦ The rewards for your efforts include greater vitality and ease of movement and less pain.

Alexander About Town

Physiologist Nicholaas Tinbergen devoted half his 1973 Nobel Prize acceptance speech to an endorsement of the Alexander Technique. Many artistic institutions have the Alexander Technique in their curricula, including Juilliard School; UCLA; Aspen Music Festival; American Conservation Theater; Royal College of Dramatic Arts. The Israeli Air Force uses the system for stress reduction and rehabilitation of injured pilots.

Alexander Movement Improvement

Exercise

THE HEAD AND NECK

- Inhibit the common impulse to tighten (shorten) the neck. This will allow your neck muscles to relax and lengthen. Think, *Head forward and up,* to encourage release and lifting.

- Have a friend very gently hold your head in her palms as you stand facing forward, eyes open. Relax the muscles in your neck. Allow your head to move forward slightly and up in relation to your neck.

- Your friend gradually lets go and moves away. Notice if you feel any taller and freer.

Alexander's Four Basic Directions

1. Think longer.

2. Think wider.

3. Let the back open.

4. Let the legs separate from the torso.

Exercise

THE SPINE

- Notice as you walk and move that your torso and spine are able to move independently from your legs.

- Do not pull down and shorten your neck, torso, and back as you walk. Imagine you can lengthen them as you move.

- Do not tighten your hip muscles. Allow the muscles around your hip joints to relax so your legs and lower back can move freely.

- Relax your buttocks muscles as you move. Tightening them can cause pressure on the sciatic nerve and thus trigger low-back pain.

- Walk allowing your head and spine to lengthen up and your legs to move freely.

BOOKS

Alexander, F. Matthias. *Constructive Conscious Control of the Individual.* Long Beach, Calif.: Centerline Press, 1985.

——, *Man's Supreme Inheritance.* Long Beach, Calif.: Centerline Press, 1989.

——, *The Resurrection of the Body.* New York: Delta, 1971.

——, *The Use of the Self.* Long Beach, Calif.: Centerline Press, 1985.

——, *The Universal Constant in Living.* Long Beach, Calif.: Centerline Press, 1986.

Barlow, Wilfred, M.D. *The Alexander Technique: How to Use Your Body Without Stress.* Rochester, Vt.: Healing Arts Press, 1990.

Caplan, Deborah, P.T. *Back Trouble: A New Approach to Prevention and Recovery Based on the Alexander Technique.* Gainesville, Fla.: Triad Publishing Company, 1987.

Connington, Bill. "The Alexander Technique: A Method for Psychophysical Change." *Massage and Bodywork Quarterly,* Vol. VIII, Issue I, Winter 1993, pp. 9–10.

Maisel, Edward, ed. *The Alexander Technique: The Essential Writings of F. Matthias Alexander.* New York: Lyle Stuart, 1990.

ORGANIZATIONS

Alexander Teaching Network
PO Box 53
UK Kendal, Cumbria LA9 4UP

North American Society of Teachers
of the Alexander Technique
PO Box 5536
Playa del Rey, CA 90296

North American Society of Teachers
of the Alexander Technique
PO Box 112484
Tacoma, WA 98411

4.

Aston-Patterning

What and When

Aston-Patterning is a system of relaxed movement and exercise designed to improve your motion range, muscle flexibility, and balance. It can be used for posture realignment and motion improvement. Usually during a session you are clothed and exercising.

Spiraling Through Space

When Judith Aston suffered major injuries in a car accident, she found it difficult to continue her exercise-teaching work with athletes and actors. Aston received physical therapy from Ida Rolf, to which she responded very well. Aston became an admirer of Rolf's work and determined to incorporate it into her own. She developed the first complete movement-education program to accompany Rolfing in 1971, which she dubbed Rolf-Aston Structural Patterning and Movement Analysis.

Over years of work Aston came to disagree with some of Rolf's key concepts, so in 1977 she started her own organization and named the new work Aston-Patterning. From her observations Aston concluded that all movement, physical and spiritual, occurs in a three-dimensional spiral pattern. In Aston-Patterning Bodywork each person's needs are considered individually, and a unique program of treatment is designed. It can include Aston Massage, Neurokinetics (movement education), Myokinetics (deep-tissue massage), and Aston Fitness exercise.

Aston-Patterning

- Emphasizes the relationship of the individual's movement to his or her environment.

- Proposes that there is no one ideal body type.

- Focuses on three-dimensional-space movement awareness.

- Is built around gentle exercises that increase a person's understanding of their patterns in movement and in relation to their surroundings.

- Aims to balance and improve all aspects of your movement performance and experience.

- *Aston-Patterning* usually refers to the movement-education part of the system, during which you learn less stressful, more efficient ways of performing everyday movements and progress to improving more complex activities such as sports and other movement performance.

The Aston-Patterning work represents a new paradigm shift in thinking about the body and movement. . . . The Aston Fitness Program for Seniors is, to my mind, the one approach to physical training for the elderly which clearly meets their needs.
—PROF. ERIK H. ERIKSON
HUMAN DEVELOPMENT, HARVARD UNIVERSITY

- As well as learning how to move well, you can receive massage, and instruction in how to alter your chairs, car seats, and exercise machines to make them better for your body.

- Aston Fitness training includes loosening through self-massage; toning exercises to increase tone and stability; stretching to move lengthening through the whole body rather than overextend one area; and cardiovascular fitness.

A Typical Aston-Patterning Session

Step 1. History

Your physical and psychological history are taken.

Step 2. Pretesting

Your practitioner observes your movement as you perform basic activities such as sitting, walking, lifting, et cetera, in order to improve your awareness and to establish a comparison for later changes. Posture charts are made.

Step 3. Movement Education and Bodywork

Movement training along with massage, myofascial release, and bone and joint tension release (Arthrokinetics) are part of all sessions.

Step 4 and Step 5. Posttesting and Applications

Pretesting movements are repeated to observe changes. These changes are applied to situations in your daily life.

Practitioner Training in Aston Therapeutics Includes

- visual assessment skills for making sense of the body's complex patterns; distinguishing between core symptoms and compensation complaints

- notation system for record keeping

- understanding asymmetry as the body's natural dynamic; listening to the body's asymmetrical pattern and matching it; keeping the whole body in balance

- engaging and empowering your client in her development; tailoring the work to her specific daily activities

- working deeply without causing pain

- effectively using your own body to remain pain free and vital

ORGANIZATIONS

Aston Training Center
PO Box 3568
Incline Village, NV 89450
Fax: (775) 831-8955

WEB SITES

AstonPat@aol.com for e-mail
www.aston-patterning.com

Can be ordered through Aston Training Center:

Aston Postural Assessment Workbook; Therapy Skill Builders, 1998

Video: *Aston Treadmill Workout,* Spring 1999

Video: *Aston Walk Your Better Body,* Spring 1999

5.

Chiropractic

What and When

Chiropractic is a system of medical healing by movement of the bones of your spine and by fairly deep muscle massage. Try it if you have a vertebra out of alignment, whiplash, or backache due to spinal misalignment. You are dressed in a hospital gown and lying on a chiropractic treatment table.

Chiropractic Capsule

"Straighten your spine" is time-tested advice. As long as 2,500 years ago Babylonian, Chinese, and Greek medical texts describe early "Chiropractic" ("done by hands") manipulation of the human muscles and bones to treat a variety of complaints. However, the modern Chiropractic system is largely the creation in the late 1800s of an American grocer, Daniel David Palmer, who became interested in magnetic healing and physical therapy. Palmer's first documented Chiropractic session was the healing of a man's deafness by realigning his neck vertebrae.

Why Is It Different?

- In contrast to Western medicine, which sees disease as the result of an invading agent, Chiropractic sees health problems as the result of imbalance of the spinal column and all the nerves, muscles, and organs it affects.

- Rather than give a patient with back pain a drug as a medical doctor usually would, a Chiropractic doctor administers a spinal manipulation.

- In Chiropractic theory, if the spine is properly aligned and flexible, the whole body will function well. X rays are taken to facilitate the doctor's understanding of the patient's spinal alignment.

- Exercise is often prescribed to prevent future problems, to train the patient to move correctly, and to strengthen the back muscles in order to hold the spine in place.

A Chiropractic Manipulation Session

- A personal interview and medical history are taken.

- A chiropractic adjustment, that is, manipulation of the spine by the doctor, is usually done. Chiropractic aims to maintain health through the stimulation of all the nerves as they leave the spinal cord.

◆ Nutrition counseling is given to maintain a level of both psychological and physical health. Digestive cleansing is used for various conditions. Chiropractics believe arthritis is caused by waste materials being deposited in the joints. The toxic buildup from the body's metabolism enlarges joints while the blood vessels narrow. Chiropractic deals with cleansing of the tissues for illnesses such as arthritis, and the adequate elimination of toxins so the metabolism is at its peak and all systems perform well.

◆ Chiropractic is presented in the schools as a preventive system to help patients maintain their well-being and resistance to disease. To assess health you consider the person's physical systems and whether she maintains the body at peak performance.

Chiropractic Help for Sleep

+ The back needs support. The spine is affected during sleep and by sleep surfaces. The firmer the bed, the better. In fact, some people with enough padding on their bones could sleep on the floor. If your back is very sore, and you don't have a good bed, you can try sleeping on the floor on several folded-up blankets for a few days.

+ If you have such a sore back that you wouldn't want to lie flat on one hip because of the pain, light movement will gradually ease it. It helps if you go on a cleansing diet, drinking some carrot or grapefruit juice and eating very light meals.

+ Lie flat without a pillow so that the tension on your spine is equalized on either side of the body. If the neck muscles are sore (but not inflamed—then you need ice) try an electric heating pad turned on low rolled just under the neck. The spine and the head should be on the same plane. This helps the body to normalize its spinal alignment.

Being Seated

+ Sit close to the table with both feet on the floor. If you hunch over to eat, you won't digest well.

+ If you have back trouble, you probably have pain sitting, sleeping, and driving, mostly due to poor posture. Car seats today have you partially lying down while driving. You sit tilted too far back so that the angle of back to hip is straight, rather than at forty-five degrees. Straighten the car seats as much as possible. Relieve the discomfort now and then by stopping and walking and stretching.

+ If you are hunched over while writing or typing, stand up, bring the shoulders back, and breathe deeply every hour. Otherwise you'll most likely become hunched permanently. Remember to take care of your back.

Note of Caution

Chiropractic is not actually a Bodywork system. It is a medical treatment. But since it is a system that includes many of the ideas and treatments used in Bodywork, it is included in this section. Also Chiropractic is many people's first experience of Bodywork techniques and leads them to be interested in more unusual Bodywork systems. Spine manipulations are the core treatments of Chiropractic. These are not safe for untrained laypersons to do. But the nutrition information and the daily preventive back-care information are things anyone can use. You can contact one of the Chiropractic professional associations for a referral to a reliable doctor.

Gentle Back-Alignment Exercises

+ A simple movement people with back problems can do is to stand tall in the morning; to stretch toward the ceiling with the fingertips, stretch up off the heels onto the toes, then come back onto the heels and lean forward over the floor without bending the knees much.

+ Next stand with the feet apart and reach one hand down toward the opposite foot, and the other hand over to the other foot.

+ Then stand up and reach toward the ceiling, taking a deep breath. Do this sequence three times, near an open window so some oxygen comes into the lungs.

+ Then you can jog gently in place for a minute or two.

ORGANIZATIONS

American Chiropractic Association
1701 Clarendon Blvd.
Arlington, VA 22209

Association for Network Chiropractic
444 West Main Street
Longmont, CA 80501

British Chiropractic Association
29 Whitley Street
UK Reading, Berks RG2 0EG

International Chiropractors Association (ICA)
1110 North Glebe Road, Suite 1000
Arlington, VA 22201

National Directory of Chiropractic
PO Box 10056
Olathe, KS 66051

World Chiropractic Alliance
2950 N. Dobson Road, Suite 1
Chandler, AZ 85224

6.
CranioSacral Therapy

What and When

CranioSacral is a subtle massage of the head and back by very light pressure. This can help jaw tension, headaches, and neck injuries. During a session you are clothed and lying down on a treatment table.

Bright Ideas

Many people think a simple head massage feels fabulous. CranioSacral Therapy explains how a scalp rub can relax your whole body. CranioSacral osteopathy began in the early 1800s as a branch of medical osteopathy (a system that maintains body manipulations can treat disease and trigger healing), but what we know today as CranioSacral Therapy derives ultimately from the groundbreaking research of Dr. John Upledger, D.O., O.M.M.

Upledger's inspiration was a flash of insight by Doctor of Osteopathy William Garner Sutherland (1873–1954) that led to his discovery of the brain pulse or the "primary respiratory mechanism." Until this discovery medical anatomy textbooks asserted that the joints, or sutures, of the skull were fused and static. Sutherland thought the joints must have a function. He discovered that they move slightly in response to the swelling and receding of the cerebrospinal fluid (CSF) manufactured by the central nervous system. He also found that the skull, spine, sacrum, and dura mater membranes around the brain and spinal cord move in response to the pulse of the cerebrospinal fluid. Sutherland learned to feel the CSF pulse and to use changes in it to diagnose the normalcy of the body's functions.

Later, Dr. John Upledger expanded this work to include manipulations of various body areas to adjust the CSF at specific places on the body and named his system of adjustments CranioSacral Therapy. His treatment focuses on releasing tension in the membrane layers surrounding the brain and the spinal cord by the use of gentle head massage and sometimes light movements of other body parts. Dr. Upledger found that treatment confined to these areas could align and relax the whole body.

A Typical CranioSacral Session

+ The client lies down on his or her back in loose clothing on a massage table.

+ The treatment is subtle and noninvasive. A CranioSacral practitioner makes small movements of the bones and soft tissues of the skull and pelvis in order to realign imbalance in other parts of the body.

+ Many people with chronic headaches, TMJ syndrome, nervous disorders, or eye problems find CranioSacral helps where other therapies fail.

+ Because child and infant skulls can be soft and still forming, it is best to confine CranioSacral Therapy to adults unless the practitioner is highly trained and professionally recommended for work on children.

Head First

- **Cerebrospinal fluid (CSF)** is enclosed in connective tissue that surrounds the brain, spinal cord, spinal column, and nerve roots. CranioSacral practitioners aim to relieve pain, muscle, and skeletal problems and nervous-system disorders (such as palsy and paralysis) by treatment focused on freeing the functioning of the cerebrospinal fluid. This CranioSacral system goes from head to tail.

- **Training and manual sensitivity** are necessary to learn to feel the CSF pulse and then to analyze its meanings. The CranioSacral practitioner's touch is extremely light in order not to disturb the subtle CSF pulse. A skilled CranioSacral practitioner can make tiny adjustments by pressing lightly on any area of the body to facilitate major postural and muscular alignments.

- **During treatment gentle pressure and movements are made** from the head down to the tip of the spine. Adjustments in the CSF pulse can release neural tension and ailments.

The CranioSacral System and Its
Relationship to Other Body Systems

The CranioSacral system may be defined as a recently recognized, functioning physiological system. The anatomic parts of the CranioSacral system are:

1. the other nonosseous connective tissue structures that are intimately related to meningeal membranes

2. all cerebrospinal fluid

3. all structures related to production, resorption, and containment of the cerebrospinal fluid

The CranioSacral system is influenced by:

1. the nervous system

2. the musculoskeletal system

3. the vascular system

4. the lymphatic system

5. the endocrine system

6. the respiratory system

Abnormalities in the structure or function of any of these systems may influence the CranioSacral system. Abnormalities in the structure or function of the CranioSacral system will necessarily have profound, and frequently deleterious, effects upon the development or function of the nervous system, especially the brain.

The CranioSacral system provides the "internal milieu" for the development, growth, and functional efficiency of the brain and spinal cord from the time of embryonic formation until death.

Brain Pulse

The CranioSacral practitioner monitors the rhythm of the cerebrospinal fluid flow just as another medical practitioner might take your wrist pulse and use it for diagnosis. A CranioSacral practitioner believes disturbances in the CSF pulse indicate larger problems, and also that balancing the CSF pulse can heal these larger physical ailments. The skulls of living people are slightly flexible at the joints where the eight bones of the skull join. It is these skull joints or sutures that the practitioner seeks to adjust to relieve imbalances in pressure in the head.

Exercise

TAKING YOUR CRANIOSACRAL PULSE

The CranioSacral pulse is the rhythm of the cerebrospinal fluid (CSF) pumping through the lining of the brain, the spinal cord, and the nerve roots coming from the spinal column. It is distinct from your cardiovascular pulse and from your breathing rhythm. It can be felt anywhere in the body. When learning the work, look for it first at the source, the head, because it is stronger there.

Hold your breath so you won't confuse CSF pulse with your breath rate or heartbeat. Gently place your hands on top of the head, yours or your partner's. Use your fingertips to sense it. This is a subtle movement that expands and contracts with the pumping of the CSF.

The CranioSacral pulse can be a reliable index for evaluating chronic debilitating conditions. It does not fluctuate, as heartbeat and breathing do, with exercise or excitement levels. The normal rhythm is six to twelve cycles per minute. If your CSF pulse varies greatly from this norm, you can use the Still Pulse exercise to help balance it.

Still Pulse Benefits

This is a good "shotgun" technique for enhancing tissue and fluid motion, especially relaxing connective tissues throughout the body, and for restoring flexibility of autonomic-nervous-system response. It is beneficial for acute and chronic musculoskeletal lesions, including degenerative arthritis. It can lower fever as much as four degrees Fahrenheit. It can reduce cerebral or pulmonary congestion, or dependent edema. It has been used to improve autoimmune disease, autistic behavior of children, and anxiety. This technique can benefit most individuals to some degree, and is rarely harmful.

Cautions
The only contraindications are in situations in which even slight and transient increases in intracranial pressure are to be avoided: impending cerebrovascular aneurysm or hemorrhage—an acute stage of stroke or cranial trauma.

—Dr. James Nelson Riley

Exercise

STILL PULSE

The CranioSacral system (CRI) in the body has a mobile rhythmic activity. Membranes (the ameningeal membranes) enclose the CranioSacral system, which includes the brain and the spinal cord, as well as the muscle and bone systems of the head, the spinal vertebrae, and the pelvis.

Momentary stillness in the CranioSacral pulse, or CRI, helps give the system a rest and a chance to balance any irregularities in its rhythm.

Major CranioSacral treatments are safe only when done by a highly trained

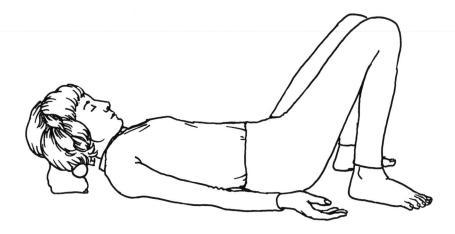

professional. However, stilling the CranioSacral pulse for a short time, from five to fifteen minutes, can be done by anyone and is very relaxing, safe, and rejuvenating for the whole body.

Place two balls in the toe of a sock, then knot it tightly. To assure that the balls stay in contact with each other, place the first sock inside another sock that is also tied tightly. Securing the balls also can be done without a sock by putting holes through the balls on a straight line and tying them together with string or leather ties.

Lie on your back, on the floor or on a sofa or bed. Place the two balls under your head so that the entire weight of your head rests on the balls. Each should be to either side of the back center of the head at the top of the occipital bone (the ridge above the neck). There is a slight depression in the skull just above the bony ridge, right above the start of the main neck muscles. (The level is slightly above that of the ear openings.)

Relax and allow the weight of your head to rest on the balls for fifteen minutes. If you need to, shift position slightly in order to maintain symmetry.

BOOKS

Upledger, John E., D.O., O.M.M. *A Brain Is Born*. Palm Beach Gardens, Fla.: The Upledger Institute, 1995.

——, *CranioSacral Therapy I: Study Guide*. Palm Beach Gardens, Fla.: The Upledger Institute, 1992.

——, *CranioSacral Therapy II: Beyond the Dura*. Seattle: Eastland Press, 1987.

——, *CranioSacral Therapy, SomatoEmotional Release: Your Inner Physician and You*. Berkeley: North Atlantic Books, and Palm Beach Gardens, Fla.: The Upledger Institute, 1991.

——, "Craniosacral Osteopathy, the Energy Cyst: Part II." *Caduceus*, No. 7, 1989, n.p.

——, and John D. Vredegvoogd, M.F.A. *CranioSacral Therapy*, Seattle: Eastland Press, 1988.

ℐ   ORGANIZATIONS   ℐ

Cranial Academy
8202 Clearvista Parkway, Suite 9D
Indianapolis, IN 46256

Upledger Institute
11211 Prosperity Farms Road
Palm Beach Gardens, FL 33410

7.

Feldenkrais

What and When

Feldenkrais is a system of precise movements designed to improve your coordination and range of movement. You are clothed and exercising in different positions. It aims to enhance your sports performance or simply improve your body alignment. It can be particularly helpful to people with serious disorders, such as Parkinson's and strokes.

A Little Move Will Do It

The Feldenkrais Method of postural realignment is a gentle system that is safe for anyone in almost any condition and can create surprisingly large positive changes. When you try the Feldenkrais Method, you may notice indications that its Russian-born originator was a physicist and an engineer as well as a serious student of Oriental martial arts. Moshe Feldenkrais is noted as the person who introduced judo to the

West by writing several books on judo and by founding the original Judo Club of France. He remained especially interested in athletes and their particular movement challenges throughout his career.

I have long been intrigued by this subtle form of retraining the nervous system, which I currently recommend to patients whose movement has been restricted by injury, cerebral palsy, stroke, fibromyalgia, or chronic pain. (I find it to be much more useful than standard physical therapy.) I also believe that the Feldenkrais Method can help older people achieve greater range of motion and flexibility, and help all of us feel more comfortable in our bodies.

—DR. ANDREW WEIL

Adult Education

As psychotherapists believe early learning is the basis for adult behavior, Moshe Feldenkrais thought that our complete adult movement pattern is learned in very early childhood. We mimic our parents' movements as infants and form body patterns in response to childhood trauma that we carry into adulthood. Then we repeat these few movement patterns over and over without expanding our repertoire or correcting bad habits.

Feldenkrais found that our movement becomes so restricted that most of us leave ninety-five percent of our movement potential unused.

The Feldenkrais exercises seek to expand the repertoire of a person's movements and to teach ways of thinking and responding by which the person can learn to free her muscle functioning from old constrictions and continue to heal injuries and bad habits throughout life.

> What I'm after isn't flexible bodies, but flexible brains.
>
> —MOSHE FELDENKRAIS, D.SC.

Functional Integration

Feldenkrais titles his work with clients in private, individual sessions "Functional Integration." The group classes are called Awareness Through Movement. Functional Integration has much in common with the work of F. Matthias Alexander, whose system Feldenkrais admired. The movements are small, precise, and gentle. Feldenkrais conceptualized that his system was retraining a person's nervous system so that he would respond in new ways to old stimuli. The Feldenkrais exercises are aimed at helping the person become conscious of previously unconscious habits. Once you notice what you are doing, you can choose to modify it in a more healthful pattern by exercising new patterns. For instance, the neck, chest, and spine exercise that follows helps you notice how you move those areas and respond with a more comfortable motion.

A Study Done at the University of Wisconsin in Milwaukee

Examining middle-aged lab rats, the researchers found that physical exercise causes a dramatic increase in the density of blood vessels in certain regions of the brain. The researchers believe that exercise may protect against age-related mental decline in humans, as memory loss and dementia are sometimes caused by impaired blood flow to the brain.

—*New Scientist*, 1/24/98

Brain Power

Feldenkrais emphasized the role of thinking in movement and in retraining our bodies. He believed in the power of pleasure as a teacher and as an indicator of correctness. Feldenkrais said that "even after doing something a million times the wrong way, doing it right even one time feels so good that the brain-body system *recognizes* it immediately as right."

Exercise

TO IMPROVE FLEXIBILITY IN YOUR NECK, CHEST, AND SPINE

Try this Feldenkrais exercise from *Discovering the Body's Wisdom* by Mirka Knaster (Bantam).

+ Sit on the front of your chair, palms resting on thighs, feet flat on the floor and shoulder width apart. Make small, gentle movements. Look to the right and turn your torso that way. Then slowly return to face forward. Notice how far you can turn without tension. Pause.

+ Next focus your eyes on a spot straight ahead and keep looking at this spot throughout this exercise. Exhale as you turn your head and torso to the right. Notice that you don't turn as far when you keep your gaze fixed straight ahead. Pause a moment.

+ Now repeat this turn to the right but turn your eye focus to the right also.

You probably can turn farther this time. Return to center position. Then turn only your shoulders and chest to the right as your head and gaze remain forward. Notice that your left shoulder moves forward as your right moves back. Return to center. Pause.

- Gently turn your eyes, head, and torso to the right. Return to center. Is turning becoming easier? Do you feel different on your right and left sides?

- Keep your feet flat on the floor as you move your left knee forward. Your lower back, shoulders, and head will turn to the right a bit. Return to center. Move your left knee forward while turning your torso and head to the right. Do you feel that moving your knee helps you turn? Do you feel a little taller? Pause to rest.

- Next repeat the entire sequence of movements to the left.

- Now alternate turning right and left a few times. Move slowly and smoothly. Notice if you feel more flexible.

- Alternate turning your hips and torso to the right and left as your eyes and head are turning in the opposite direction. Pause.

- Now move your left knee forward as you turn right. Then do the same to the left. Notice if your flexibility and range have increased without strain or stretch. How do you feel when you stand?

Exercise

NECK AND UPPER-BACK RELEASE

- Lie down on your back on a firm bed or on a mat on the floor. Your arms rest spread open at your sides. Your knees are bent. Position your head, spine, and hips in a straight line. Notice where you feel your spine touching the ground and where you feel it held away from the floor. Feel the weight of your head on the floor.

- As you inhale, gently roll your head to the right side, as far as you can without any muscle resistance in your neck or shoulders. This may be only a few inches. Exhale as you roll your head back to center.

- Rest a breath in the center without moving.

- Then roll your head to the left as you inhale, only as far as is easy with no resistance. Exhale as you roll your head back to center. Rest a breath in the center without moving.

- Now include your arms in the movement. Inhale as you roll your head to the right and also fold your left arm over your chest. Lift the arm at the shoulder joint. Your left hand will lightly touch your right arm as you fold. Keep the hands below shoulder height to avoid neck tension.

- As you move your arms, notice where the movement begins: in the muscles on either side of the spine between the shoulder blades.

- Roll your left arm and your head back to center. Rest a breath here.

- Roll your head to the left as you inhale and fold your right arm over your chest.

- Exhale as you roll both back to center.

- Continue this side-to-side motion gently, slowly, and smoothly.

- This motion helps relax neck and shoulder tension. Rest in the center without moving. Notice how your spine is lying on the ground. Is any more of your spine or neck touching the ground than when you began? If so, this means that your motion has relaxed the muscles' cramping and they have lengthened. Try the head roll by itself. Can you move farther to each side without strain than when you began?

BOOKS

Alon, Ruthy. *Mindful Spontaneity.* Prism/Avery, 1990.

Feldenkrais, Moshe, D.Sc. *Awareness Heals: The Feldenkrais Method for Dynamic Health.* Steven Shafarman, Addison-Wesley, 1997.

———. *Awareness Through Movement: Easy-to-Do Health Exercises to Improve Your Posture, Vision, Imagination, & Personal Awareness.* San Francisco: Harper & Row, 1972.

Rywerant, Yochanan. *The Feldenkrais Method.* Keats, 1991.

Zemach-Bersin, David et al. *Relaxercise: Ten Effortless Techniques for a More Flexible, Energetic, Pain-Free, Stress-Free Body.* San Francisco: HarperCollins, 1990.

TAPES/VIDEOS

The Feldenkrais Guild will mail you a catalog of audiocassettes and videotapes that feature a wide variety of Feldenkrais training.

ORGANIZATIONS

The Feldenkrais Guild
524 Ellsworth Street
PO Box 489
Albany, OR 97321

WEB SITES

www.feldenkrais.com

Massage: Swedish

8

What and When

Swedish Massage is a comfortable, therapeutic muscle rubdown with oil. Usually you keep on your underwear. Try a session when you have mild muscle strain, sports injury, or need light physical therapy.

Starting with the Swedes

Ahhh, massage. It's wonderful that something that feels so good really is a therapeutic treatment. Today such a wide variety of exotic Body Therapy techniques is available in most communities that the power and benefits of basic massage can be overlooked.

Massage is medicine.

—JAMES GORDON, M.D., PH.D.

Although forms of massage have been in use for thousands of years, from Egypt to China to Greece, massage for Western medical treatment was organized and popularized more recently in Sweden in the 1800s. Sir Per Henrik Ling started the Royal Institute of Gymnastics in Stockholm in 1813 with the goal of training others in his unique combination of physical-therapy movements with medically tested circulation-stimulation techniques, including some influence from Asian martial arts.

Ling developed his work, which later became known simply as Swedish Massage, from trying to cure his own rheumatoid arthritis. He devised muscle-manipulation techniques that would help circulation, release muscle tension, ease sore joints, and improve nerve functioning as well as bolster the patient's overall sense of well-being by triggering the body's production of its natural opiates. Swedish massage is made up of specific strokes aimed at improving medical problems. The strokes usually focus on one area of the body at a time and are performed vigorously.

To Do or Not To Do

Massage is not advisable if you have any kind of infection, clotting, or skin disorder, including cancer, because the rubbing may spread it. No deep massage should be given directly on any injured or painful area. Massage around the area to relax the patient.

In general the benefits you may expect are pain and stress reduction, improved circulation, and heightened physical performance due to the release of tense muscles. Massage in the medical arena is used often to relax a person before and after uncomfortable treatments and to speed healing by reducing stress.

Massage can help [a sprain] recover in one third the normal time. In more serious instances, like muscular dystrophy and various forms of spastic and flaccid paralysis, massage can help retard muscle atrophy.

—JILL THOMPSON, PATHOLOGY INSTRUCTOR, SWEDISH INSTITUTE

A Typical Swedish Session

A typical Swedish Massage session lasts from thirty minutes to one hour. Unless you or your doctor requests that the therapist focus on a particular area, the treatment will cover your entire body. You can wear your underwear. You lie down on a massage table with a sheet or large towel for cover. The therapist applies massage oil (often mineral oil based) to your skin so that the rubbing will not cause uncomfortable friction. Some Swedish Massages include heat packs and water therapy. The cost varies, but a typical range is between $50 and $90 per hour.

Swedish Massage Strokes

Swedish Massage strokes are fun and useful to learn so that you can give loved ones TLC. Here are the basic types:

+ **Compression**—rhythmic pumping on a muscle to help it relax and to increase circulation, which helps wash out metabolic wastes.

+ **Effleurage**—stroking that glides over the body. Work rhythmically with palms, thumbs, fingertips, or forearms for a soothing effect or with deep pressure toward the heart to stimulate circulation.

+ **Friction**—rubbing in circular, linear, or transverse strokes on the surface of the skin. Deeper pressure penetrates to the superficial fascia to spread the muscle fibers and free muscles from adhesions and scar tissue formed after an injury.

+ **Petrissage**—kneading rhythmically, lifting muscles from the bone, then squeezing and rolling them. Use both hands or both thumbs to grasp the tissue in a continuous movement while traveling along an arm, a shoulder, or the back.

Combinations, Reversals, and Functions

While giving a massage you can invent a new stroke by combining two old ones if they work well together. Combined strokes feel different to the receiver because they take in larger areas and give the receiver a different awareness of her body. For instance, receiving a circular stroke on the palm of your hand and next a circular stroke on the arch of your foot gives a very different sensation from the combined stroke of having both areas massaged simultaneously. You can also experiment with reversing the direction of a stroke. Stay aware of the function, as well as the shape, of a body part. This will help you give a massage that complements the muscles' natural movement. For example, when massaging the shoulders, strokes moving up toward the neck and down toward the tailbone feel better than ones moving from spine to shoulder joint. Of course, studying anatomy can help define your strokes.

+ **Range of motion**—passive moving of limbs to increase flexibility, rotate, flex, and extend the body parts.

+ **Tapotement**—delivering percussive movements in short, rapid strokes only to the fleshy parts of the body. Hack with the outside edge of the hand. Tap with the fingertips. Cup or clap with cupped palms and the fingers close together. Pummel with loose fists. In plucking, practitioners pick up small patches of flesh or loosely pinch them between the thumb and fingertips. These strokes have a stimulating or toning effect when used for a few seconds. It is not advisable to use them longer, as they can lead to exhaustion of nerves and muscles.

+ **Vibration**—using hands or fingertips to create a rapid trembling, shaking sensation and stimulate nerves and release tense muscles.

They could not live without petting.

—EMPEROR FREDERICK II OF GERMANY

13TH CENTURY; COMMENT ON DEATHS OF NEGLECTED INFANTS IN ORPHANAGES

Swedish Massage Strokes

Exercise

HACKING ON THE BACK

One of the tapotement Swedish strokes is Hacking, which, when done well, feels much better than it might sound. It is the stroke you probably saw done to a boxer in a 1940s movie when the trainer pummeled the athlete's back after a tough match. You can do it more gently. With your thumbs up and your fingers held together, alternating hands, use the outer 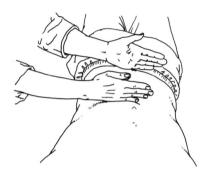 edges of both hands to drum rhythmically on the long back muscles on either side of the spine. Work from shoulders to hips and then back up. You can also continue down and up the legs. This stimulates circulation in the muscles.

Exercise

VIBRATING THE BUTTOCKS

Vibration Swedish style can be done on any large muscle. Try it on some of the largest. Spread the fingers of your right hand wide open and taut. Place your palm on the lower slopes of both buttocks at once and slightly lean into your hand. Then shake your hand quickly from side to side, keeping your hand in place firmly and vibrating the buttocks muscles. This can be very relaxing for the hips and the lower back.

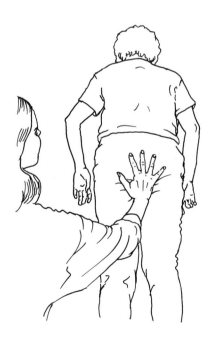

MOVING THE KNEE

Moving passive limbs to increase range of motion in the joints is a pleasant part of Swedish Massage. While your friend is lying on his or her stomach, place one palm under the ankle and the other under the shin. Lift the foreleg and bend it at the knee. The thigh rests on the table. Slowly lean a bit of weight on the foreleg so that the heel moves toward the buttock. Only go as far as is comfortable to the receiver. Then slowly lower the foreleg to the table. Repeat with the other leg.

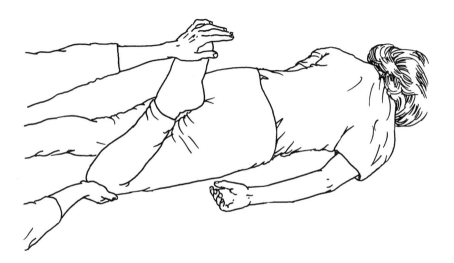

Massage: Esalen

9

What and When

Esalen Massage is a soothing rubdown with oil that combines muscle relaxation with verbal emotional therapy. Usually you are nude, but this is optional. Try a session when you feel stressed and in need of psychophysical renewal.

Rubbing the Right Way

California has a reputation for changing how people do things, and this holds true for its effect on massage. In California, Swedish Massage slowed down and shifted its focus from medical therapy to sensual communication. Esalen Institute in Big Sur, California, has been the center in the United States of a variety of leading-edge explorations in psychotherapy and human development that have resulted in the formation of new schools of thought and practice. Many of these developments are of interest only to specialized therapists and academics. However, Esalen Massage has

> Massage is for your mate, your family, and your friends. It is for grandmothers
> and babies, for pets, for those you love, and, if you are up to it, for those you hate.
> To do massage is physically to help someone, to take care of them. It is for anyone
> with whom you feel prepared to share an act of physical healing.
>
> —GEORGE DOWNING, *THE MASSAGE BOOK*

become so popular and pervasive in mainstream culture that it is hard to imagine life in the U.S.A. without it.

Massage has long been a respected part of health care and luxury relaxation in Europe and in Asia. But until the 1970s, massage in the United States was relegated to sex parlors and physical therapy. In the late 1960s body therapists at Esalen Institute combined the muscle therapy strokes of Swedish Massage with newly developed sensory-awareness techniques at Esalen to give birth to a sensual form of massage uniting emotional awareness with physical relaxation.

George Downing, a therapist working at Esalen in the early 1970s, wrote a book on how to do Esalen Massage, offering techniques to the general public and not restricting the information to medical workers. *The Massage Book* (Random House) became a best-seller and has inspired continuing offspring of further massage manuals in a field where there were none before. The book recently came out in its twenty-fifth anniversary edition and is still the classic text for Esalen Massage.

Enjoying a relaxing, light massage usually leads to experimenting with the harder stuff. If massage makes a person feel so good, why not try other Bodywork? Massage's popularity piqued interest in other Esalen techniques, and spread esoteric Body

Doing is inspiring. While massaging, your hands naturally invent patterns if you relax and let them, so experiment. Also pay attention to any responses from the person you are massaging for ideas for inventing new strokes. Another way to invent a stroke is to make up a name and create a stroke that fits it. What stroke would fit the title "sculpting"?

Therapies out of the world of professional therapists and into the everyday lives of average Americans.

Comparing Swedish and Esalen Methods

In comparison to Swedish Massage Esalen Massage is very sensual, employing longer strokes and often using scented oils. A Swedish masseur traditionally would talk little during the massage and would not encourage emotional feedback. The receiver of an Esalen massage is encouraged to be aware of his or her reactions to the various physical experiences and to share any emotional responses with the masseur. Attention is paid not only to the emotional and physical responses of the recipient, but also to the comfort and sensory experience of the giver. The masseur makes sure he is in a comfortable position while working and does not strain his back.

Close your eyes while giving a massage. This will decrease outside distractions and increase your ability to "think with your hands." With your eyes closed you are guided by touch rather than by sight and are more likely to work sensitively.

Esalen Massage strokes are designed to improve a person's body awareness. Some strokes extend from head to toe in order to give the receiver a physical sense of connectedness and unity. Smaller strokes may be used not only to release muscle tension in a specific area, but also to enlarge a person's idea of the unexpected sensuality of an ignored area. For instance, most people find the Esalen Massage strokes for the ears and the knees surprisingly sensual. Other Esalen Massage techniques are aimed at giving the person a heightened awareness of her shape and structure. Learning Esalen Massage, you are encouraged to let your fingers carefully define each body structure as though you are sculpting the shape. And you are encouraged to invent your own new strokes in response to the individual.

While Swedish Massage is intended to promote physical health by manipulation of the soft tissues of the body, Esalen Massage is designed as a technique to integrate a person's awareness of body and mind. The aim is to unite the two aspects of ourselves so that we function more comfortably and effectively.

A body part's contour demands individual treatment tailored to its shape. As you massage a knee or a calf, for instance, you'll find that your hands naturally mold themselves around the bone and the muscle. Different movements feel more comfortable on bony areas than on muscular areas. Part of the pleasure of a good massage is clarifying your sense of the unique shape of your body.

An Esalen Session

A typical Esalen Massage session lasts from one hour to as long as two hours. The client is nude (or in underwear if desired) and lies down on a sheet on a massage table. The masseur or masseuse applies vegetable massage oil to the skin so that the strokes will feel smooth and the client's skin will receive healthful nutrients. The client is encouraged to inform the masseuse of any personal preferences and to share any emotional reactions during the massage. The massage covers the entire body and is done flowingly, like a dance. The comfort of both the giver and the receiver is considered part of the process. The masseuse pays close attention to her posture to prevent back strain and experiments with new strokes to keep a spontaneous feel to the massage. The cost varies from $50 to $100 and up, often higher in larger cities.

Contrary to myth, massage is a healing art and not an advanced sexual technique.
Naturally, when practiced by lovers, it can be a beautiful extension of sexuality.
The flowing peace and aliveness it so easily brings to the body can be
channeled, if both parties desire things so, in that direction. But this is
merely one of many possibilities that massage holds out to us.
The core of massage lies in its unique way of communicating without words. . . .
Trust, empathy, and respect, to say nothing of a sheer sense of physical existence,
for this moment can be expressed with a fullness never matched
by words. . . . It makes us more whole.

—GEORGE DOWNING

Esalen Massage Strokes for the Back

There is no pleasure quite like that of a good back massage. Combining the medical benefits of physical therapy and the comfort of a mother's caring, with the stimulation of a sensual treat, the back rub seems to rate high on everybody's list of favorite things. As body therapy, back rubs are soothing because a complex system of nerves radiates from the spinal cord to almost every part of the body, and by massaging the back nerves you can relax your whole body. Massage can improve circulation, relax tight muscles, and release rigid connective tissues. You can ease tension throughout the body by relaxing the back.

Receiving a back rub is often experienced as a luxury because touching the back can be sensual without being demandingly sexual. And giving can be as pleasurable as receiving as one delves into the lovely planes and valleys of one of the largest expanses of smooth skin and muscle in the human form.

Exercise

SIDE STROKES

Carefully spread warm massage oil all over your partner's back. Use just enough to make your hand strokes smooth across the skin, but not so much that the body feels

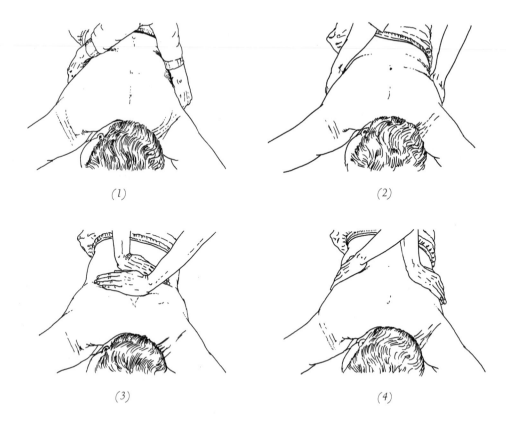

(1)   (2)

(3)   (4)

gooey or too slippery for good hand contact. Kneel or stand to one side of the person's hips. Begin palms down with the heels of your hands resting on the table to either side of your partner's upper back and fingertips pointing toward the spine. Slide your fingertips toward each other. Just before they touch at the spine, move your hands slightly away from each other so that they can continue all the way down your partner's sides again to the table.

Now reverse the motion by sliding the heels of your hands back to the starting position. Repeat this cross-over stroking up and down your partner's back from the shoulders down the back to the hips.

Exercise

THE WATERFALL

Stand to the left of your partner's hips. Begin at the top of the spine with the tips of the first two fingers of your right hand pressing into the muscles on either side of the vertebrae. Slide your fingertips about two or three inches down the muscles on either side of the spine. Then begin the same pressing, sliding motion with the first two fingertips of your left hand, covering again the area of spinal muscles that your right hand has covered. Lift your right hand and slide the fingers of your left hand an inch or so farther down the back than your right hand. Now slide the fingertips of your right hand a few inches farther down the back. Keep repeating this alternating sliding and pressing with your fingertips on both sides of the spine. As one set of fingertips is pressing, raise the other off the back. Then start the motion with your other hand. On the receiving end this overlapping stroke, rhythmically done, will feel as if something soothing, like a waterfall, is rolling down your back.

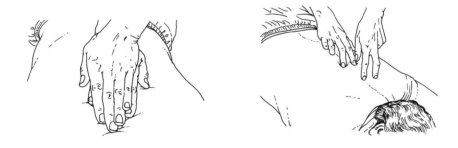

Try massaging with a part of your hand or arm you've not used for massage be-fore. Some wonderful long strokes for the back can be done with the inside of your fore-arm. Your fists and knuckles can feel good when dragged along the muscles of a well-oiled back. Turn your hand palm-up and try lightly sliding your fingernails from shoulder to ankle in overlapping strokes.

Oils and Powders

Play with Your Food

You can mix massage oils yourself by combining the vegetable oil of your choice with a few drops of your favorite scent-essence oil. Pharmacies, groceries, and health-food stores carry these. Hand lotion and baby oil are not recommended for massage because they are sticky, probably contain petroleum, and are absorbed too quickly into the skin. You want a lubricant that keeps on lubricating. Vegetable oils fill this bill, adding nutrients as well as moisture. Safflower and almond oils are particularly pleasant under your hands.

The use of oil in massage will allow the giver to employ a wide variety of strokes—sliding across muscles, creating smooth waves of pressure, covering large distances—as well as add a sensuous quality, if desired. Keep your nails very short for your friend's comfort.

Perhaps the receiver is not ready to be anointed with oil. You can use a clay base powder from a health-food store or body and bath shop (not talcum—it clogs pores). This will give your hands some stroke lubricant to avoid unpleasant friction from dry hands. Sprinkle it on from the jar.

A plastic squeeze-top bottle makes a convenient, portable massage oil container. A small bowl into which you can dip your fingers looks prettier but may be less convenient. If your friend is tall and you place the bowl near his or her head, when you've made your way down to the foot massage, the oil bowl is probably out of reach.

Sensuous Shopping List

Fine Massage Vegetable Oils, Combined or Pure

Almond

Avocado

Coconut

Safflower

Sunflower

Delicious Fragrance Oils

Almond

Chocolate

Cinnamon

Lavender

Mint

Musk

Peach

Rose

Sandalwood

Skin Treats to Mix by the Teaspoon in Your Massage Oil

Vitamin E Oil—for removing discolorations

Aloe Vera—for healing skin cracks, scabs, and allergy rashes

Lanolin—for moisturizing

Primrose Oil—for toning

Na-PCA—for smoothing wrinkles

Honey—for tightening pores

The Big Picture: Designing a Massage

When you have learned a basic repertoire of strokes, keep these guidelines in mind to help structure a complete, satisfying massage:

- **Start slowly** and gradually work up to speedier rhythms.

- **Begin with large-scale** strokes and then proceed with details on smaller areas.

- **Include gradual transition moves** between strokes so that the whole massage feels like one long, continuous stroke to the receiver.

- **Start with light** and move gradually into heavier pressure. This allows the receiver to become accustomed to your touch.

- **Listen to feedback.** Do only what the receiver likes. Appreciate the new information. Even try using it to invent new aspects to your massage.

- **When lifting and moving a limb,** move only in its natural direction and to its range of comfort. Encourage the person to give over all the work of movement to your hands.

- **As you near the close of the massage,** gradually slow down your pace.

- **To close,** perform some strokes that cover large areas, even the whole length of the body, to leave the receiver with a sense of physical connectedness and wholeness.

- **Have fun.** The massage is for both people's pleasures.

BOOKS

American Massage Therapy Association (AMTA). *A Guide to Massage Therapy in America.* Evanston, Ill.: AMTA, 1993.

Ashley, Martin, J.D., L.M.T. *Massage: A Career at Your Fingertips.* Barrytown, N.Y.: Station Hill Press, 1992.

Burt, Bernard. *Fodor's Healthy Escapes: 244 Resorts and Retreats Where You Can Get Fit, Feel Good, Find Yourself, and Get Away from It All.* New York: Random House, Updated regularly.

Downing, George. *The Massage Book Twenty-fifth Anniversary Edition.* New York: Random House, 1999.

Knaster, Mirka. *Discovering the Body's Wisdom.* New York: Bantam Books, 1996.

Lacroix, Nitya. *Massage for Total Stress Release: The Art of Relieving Tension Through Massage.* New York: Random House, 1990.

Leboyer, Frederic. *Loving Hands: The Traditional Indian Art of Baby Massage.* New York: Alfred A. Knopf, 1976.

Maanun, Armand, and Herb Montgomery. *A Complete Book of Swedish Massage.* New York: Harper & Row, 1988.

Montagu, Ashley, Ph.D. *Touching: The Human Significance of the Skin,* 3rd ed. New York: Harper & Row, 1986.

Rush, Anne Kent. *The Back Rub Book.* New York: Vintage, 1989.

———. *Romantic Massage.* New York: Avon, 1991.

Tappan, Frances M. *Healing Massage Techniques: Holistic, Classic, and Emerging Methods.* Norwalk, Conn.: Appleton & Lange, 1988.

ORGANIZATIONS

Note: Training for massage varies from state to state. Contact some of these professional organizations for information on training and regulations in your area.

American Massage Therapy Association
820 Davis Street, Suite 100
Evanston, IL 60201–4444

Associated Bodywork and Massage Professionals
28677 Buffalo Park Road
Evergreen, CO 80439–7347

The Association of Massage Practitioners
Flat 3
52 Redcliffe Square
London SW10 9HQ
UK

International Massage Association and National Association of Massage Therapy
3000 Connecticut Avenue, NW, Suite 102
Washington, DC 20008

National Association of Nurse Massage Therapists
1720 Willow Creek Circle, #517
Eugene, OR 97402

Touch Research Institute
University of Miami
School of Medicine
PO Box 016820
Miami, FL. 33101

VIDEOS

Esalen Massage $30.00	Easlen Institute, Big Sur, Calif.
Infant Massage For new babies $19.98	Living Arts Catalog Tel: (800) 254-8464
Massage for Beginners A Cayce-Reilly Massage Video Workshop	ARE Bookstore Tel: (800) 723-1112@ep
Massage for Every Body Increase Video Company	Wishing Well Distribution
Massage for Health (Healing Arts Home Video) Hosted by Shari Belafonte $14.98	Living Arts Catalog Tel: (800) 254-8464
Pregnancy Massage For expecting parents $24.98	Living Arts Catalog Tel: (800) 254-8464

WEB SITES

Alternative Medicine Homepage
www.pitt.edu/cbw/altm.html

Holistic Internet Resources
www.hir.com

Yahoo! Alternative Medicine
www.yahoo.com/health/alternative_medicine
Links to numerous indices, organizations, and practitioners of various alternative
health modalities.

Spa-Finders Travel Arrangements
91 Fifth Avenue
Suite 301
New York, NY 10003–3039

Spa Trek Travel
475 Park Avenue South
New York, NY 10016

10.

Myotherapy

What and When

Myotherapy is a system of deep, sometimes painful pressure-point massage aimed at erasing specific areas of pain in the body to improve ease of movement. Usually you wear your underwear and lie down on a Body Therapy table.

On Target for Good Health

Myotherapy is the child of Trigger-Point Therapy popularized by Janet Travell, M.D., and the grandchild of Acupressure. Following Dr. Travell, exercise expert Bonnie Prudden promoted and popularized Myotherapy.

- ◆ The trigger points are mainly Acupuncture points, plus a few added ones.

- Trigger points are located at tender spots in tight muscles on the client's body that radiate or refer pain to other areas and limit flexibility and range of motion.

- The therapist applies moderate pressure to the sore trigger point with his or her finger until the tight muscle releases. Gradually the related pain will dissolve.

Senator Barry Goldwater claimed President John F. Kennedy's highest gift to the American people was bringing Dr. Janet Travell's work in Trigger-Point Therapy to wide public attention.

Exercise

EASING LOWER-BACK PAIN

The trigger points for lower-back pain are in the area of the back pockets of a person's jeans—usually three or four to a "pocket." The subject strips down to light exercise pants or underwear and lies on the table facedown. The muscles targeted are in the buttocks (gluteals), more specifically the gluteus maximus.

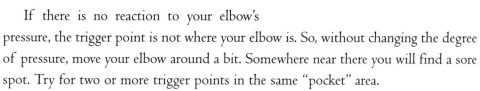

Reach across the body to gain leverage and place your elbow where the pocket would be. Slowly apply pressure. The pressure should not be straight down but angled back toward you. If your subject reacts, you have found a trigger point. Hold the pressure on that spot for seven seconds. Slowly withdraw your elbow.

If there is no reaction to your elbow's pressure, the trigger point is not where your elbow is. So, without changing the degree of pressure, move your elbow around a bit. Somewhere near there you will find a sore spot. Try for two or more trigger points in the same "pocket" area.

SIDE-LYING STRETCH

If a muscle has been in a shortened, tense position so long it is unable to let go, you have to help it. You can show it how to relax by stretching it. Have your friend roll over onto one side, *slowly*. The muscle you have just cleared is so confused that a sudden movement might cause it to jump back into the same cramp.

This exercise stretches the gluteals you have just massaged. It also stretches the muscles all down the back. Do these exercises slowly and with a rhythm. Muscles listen to rhythm. Draw the top knee up to the chest. Extend the leg straight down about eight inches above the bottom leg. Rest the top leg on the bottom leg. Relax for a slow count of three.

If your subject points the toes, this is not good because it tightens the leg muscles. Do this exercise four times. Cross over to your subject's other side and massage the other "pocket." Then repeat the exercise with the other leg.

Exercise

ERASING TRIGGER POINTS FROM HIPS

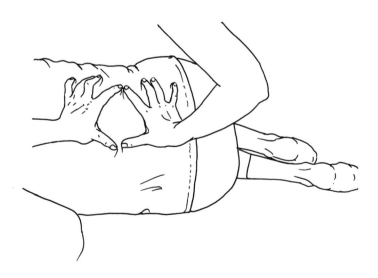

The gluteus medius muscle is on either side of the pelvis. Pressure for this muscle must be applied straight down, not at an angle to the body. Since there is less flesh, less pressure will be required. Have the subject lie on his or her side with the knees slightly bent. Search out trigger points, usually three between the waist and the bottom line of the subject's briefs. Hold the pressure in each spot for seven seconds.

Exercise

CROSS-LEG STRETCH

The subject remains in the same position. Press the top leg forward and down to stretch the gluteus medius and the muscle along the outside of the thigh. Place one of your hands on the crest of the subject's pelvis at the waist, and with the other, press down on the knee in eight short, easy bounces. When you have cleared both sides of trigger points and done the Cross-Leg Stretch on both sides, go back and repeat the Side-Lying Stretch.

FOR PAIN IN MUSCLES OF THE BACK

Most people with back pain are sure the trouble is in the spine. The truth is that it rarely is. Bones can't go anywhere by themselves. It's muscles that make them work. When muscles contract, they pull. The muscles that can cause trouble in the back are so numerous that it really makes more sense to consider them first, not the twenty-four little vertebrae that catch all the blame.

Exercise

ERASING TRIGGER POINTS FROM THE "BELT" AREA OR WAIST

Stand or sit with your hands at your waist, thumbs facing forward, fingers touching your spine, and palms flat on your back. Arch your back slightly. As the back muscles contract, there will be two bulges of muscle, one in the palm of each hand. Work on both sides of each of those bulges and each time toward the middle of the bulge.

Have your subject lie on the table, facedown. Think of your subject's "belt" as studded with four stars on each side. The first star (trigger point) you will examine is on the outside of one of those bulges about four inches from the spine, away from the muscle to be searched. Reach across your subject's body and place your elbow against the far side of the muscle. Press down and pull toward you as if trying to get in under the bulge of the muscle.

The second star to be worked is next to the spine. Place your elbow against the bulge and push down and outward. Move your elbow about one inch outward on the same horizontal belt line and repeat what you did with the first star. Press down and pull toward you.

The last spot is on the muscle called the "external oblique," on the side away from you. It requires a slightly different technique. This spot is just below the rib cage and just above the bony rim of the pelvis and is very vulnerable in any twisting action, which is required in most spots. Reach across the back and about halfway down the side toward the table. Then pull toward you and up. This is the only upward motion you ever use with your elbow.

When you have "cleared" one side of the belt area, you will need to stretch the muscles with the Cat Horse exercise.

Exercise

CAT HORSE STRETCH

Have your subject get on hands and knees and press the back upward like an angry cat while dropping the head down. Next, let the back fall in as though it belonged to a

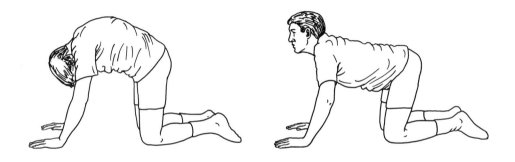

tired old sway-backed horse. Bring the head up and be sure the arms are still straight. Do this exercise four times, always slowly and with great concentration, searching out all the tight spots that need to be stretched.

The sciatic nerve is pinched in most cases not by the spine, but by a muscle in spasm. The last island of trouble in the waist area is above the belt between the second and third stars. Use the same type of pressure as that used for the second waist spot when you pressed down and pulled toward you.

Exercise

THE LIMBERING SERIES

This exercise program is a must for all ex–back sufferers. When your back is no longer a bother, add this complete series of back-limbering exercises to your daily routine. If you are on maintenance with this series (which means you no longer have pain), do one complete series morning and night.

I. Supine Stretch

Lie on your back with knees bent and arms resting at your sides. Raise your head and bring the left knee as close to your nose as you can. Help the stretch with your hands. Lie back and stretch the right leg out straight about ten inches above the bed or floor. Return to the beginning position and relax for three seconds. Do the exercise four times on each side.

2. Side-Lying Stretch

Roll over onto your right side in a relaxed position. Draw the left knee up close to your chest. Stretch the leg down, parallel with the resting leg and about eight inches above it. Lower the leg and rest for three seconds. Repeat four times.

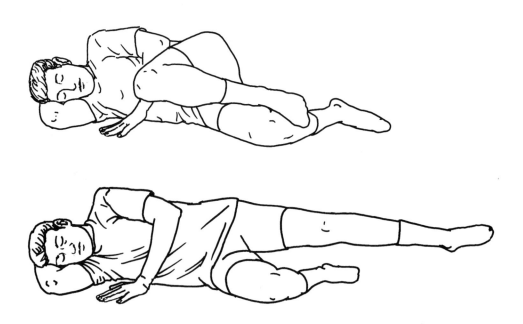

3. Prone Gluteal and Abdominal Set

Roll over onto your stomach, with your head resting on your bent arms. Tighten your seat muscles (gluteals) and your abdominals. Hold for five seconds, then relax for three seconds. Repeat three more times.

4. Supine Pelvic Tilt

On your back, with knees bent and feet about eighteen inches apart, arch the back slightly, keeping both seat and shoulders touching the floor. Then press the spine down hard while tilting the pelvis under as far as possible. Hold the tilt for five seconds and relax. Repeat four times.

BOOKS

Barnes, John. "Myofascial Release." *Physical Therapy Forum,* Sept. 16, 1987.

Prudden, Bonnie. *Myotherapy: Bonnie Prudden's Guide to Pain-Free Living.* New York: Ballantine Books, 1985.

———. *Pain Erasure: The Bonnie Prudden Way.* New York: Ballantine Books, 1985.

Travell, Janet G., M.D., and David G. Simons, M.D. *Myofascial Pain and Dysfunction: the Trigger Point Manual.* Baltimore: Williams and Wilkins, 1983.

ORGANIZATIONS

Bonnie Prudden Pain Erasure
7800 E. Speedway Boulevard
Tucson, AZ 85710

WEB SITES

www.betterhealth.com
The Better Health channel in the iVillage network offers information on recent medical research, a chat room, and even a free virtual checkup.

11.

Rolfing

What and When

Rolfing is a system of extremely deep tissue massage without oil. The practitioner works with his or her fingers, elbows, and knuckles. It can be quite painful. The aim is to release tension in stiff connective tissue or muscle frozen from trauma in order to realign posture. Usually you are nude or wearing underwear and lying down on a low Bodywork table.

Stretching It

Ida Rolf, the originator of Rolfing, was a New Yorker and invented a Bodywork system with many of the charms and challenges of her hometown. The system works, but it's tough. Rolfing, or Structural Integration, as Dr. Rolf named it, can be quite painful and is based on the premise that to change your posture and clear up problematic memories that cause current stress, one must endure forceful, deep

Beauty is an intuitive appreciation of normalcy. . . . Integration of structure is the key.

—DR. IDA P. ROLF, PH.D.

massage of the muscles and the connective tissue to ply apart fused and shortened body tissues that tilt the posture out of alignment.

Connective tissue, or fascia, forms a sheath to help support all the body's muscles, bones, and organs. But if this strong sheath becomes too rigid or is pulled too far in one direction, it can cause imbalance in the body's structure and constriction in the blood and oxygen supply to the stiffened area. The aim of Rolfing is to heat and stretch the stiffened connective tissues so that any unbalanced pulling releases and the muscles can return to their relaxed length. Then the whole body can assume its natural balanced posture.

Don't Fight Gravity

Ida Rolf believed that gravity is "man's name for the energy of the earth." Since gravity's energy is much bigger than one person's, each of us needs to learn to work with its force rather than contradict it or ignore it. Dr. Rolf said that gravity is "the never-sleeping therapist and teacher." The downward pull of gravity on our bodies can shorten our muscles and pull us out of alignment unless we continuously renew our proper alignment by correct movement, emotional balance, and deep-tissue massage.

Be ready for noticeable changes. Greta Garbo is said to have considered suing Dr. Rolf because she thought the treatments changed the shape of her famous face.

What conditions must be fulfilled in order for the human body to be organized and integrated in gravity so that it can function in the most economical way?

—DR. ROLF ON BEGINNING HER PIONEERING WORK

A Typical Rolfing Session

- To determine if you are in proper alignment, the Rolfer checks your posture.

- A photograph is taken to see whether a plumb line would make a straight course if dropped from the head to the feet, crossing through the ears, shoulder joints, hip joints, knees, and ankles on the way. More photos are taken as you move through the Rolfing sessions so you can note your progress toward proper alignment.

- Rolfing's original sequence is a series of about ten massage sessions, usually a week or so apart. Lying on a massage or low Bodywork table, you receive slow, gliding, deep strokes, with no oil, on various body areas.

- If you have memories that surface related to your Rolfed body area, these are discussed briefly with the Rolfer.

- The ten treatment sessions are followed by several lessons in Rolfing Movement Integration to teach the client how to move well.

- Then the client has the option of five treatments in the Advanced Rolfing Series.

The Focus of Rolfing's First Ten Sessions

Rolfers focus their deep-tissue massage on specific parts of the body in a systematic scheme and order, but variations are made to suit the individual's needs. Your photo is taken before and after each session to note changes and to update your body image.

- **Sessions One, Two, and Three:** The extremities plus the fascia layer just below the skin.

> Strength that has effort in it is not what you need; you need
> the strength that is the result of ease.
>
> —DR. IDA P. ROLF, PH.D.

Session One: The chest, to open breathing and circulation.

Session Two: The feet and ankles, to secure your gravitational foothold.

Session Three: Arms and legs, to connect the extremities.

✦ **Sessions Four, Five, Six, and Seven:** These four sessions focus on the deeper fascia of the body, plus the midsection of the body and the back.

✦ **Sessions Eight, Nine, and Ten:** These last three sessions focus on integrating the body, on relating all the parts in functioning, and on any special needs of the individual. **Please Note:** Rolfing is a drastic treatment that can be implemented only by a well-trained certified Rolfing practitioner.

Rolfing Research

Studies by Dr. Valerie Hunt at UCLA show that Rolfing leads to more efficient use of the muscles, more refined movement patterns, and more ability by the body to conserve energy. Studies at the University of Maryland show that Rolfing improves neurological functioning, reduces chronic stress, and improves spinal structure.

✍ BOOKS ✍

Bond, Mary. *Rolfing Movement Integration: A Self-Help Approach to Balancing the Body.* Rochester, Vt.: Healing Arts Press, 1993.

Hunt, Valerie V., Ph.D. et al. *A Study of Structural Integration from Neuromuscular, Energy Field, and Emotional Approaches.* Boulder: Rolf Institute, 1977.

Johnson, Don. *The Protean Body: A Rolfer's View of Human Flexibility.* New York: Harper & Row, 1977.

Kirby, Ron, Ph.D. "The Probable Reality Behind Structural Integration: How Gravity Supports the Body." Boulder: Rolf Institute, n.d.

Rolf, Ida. *Rolfing: Reestablishing the Natural Alignment and Structural Integration of the Human Body for Vitality and Well-Being.* Rochester, Vt.: Healing Arts, 1989.

Rolf Institute. *The Rolfing Technique of Connective Tissue Manipulation.* Boulder: Rolf Institute, 1976.

Sant'Anna, Doris, and Frank Hanenkrat, Ph.D. *The Rolfing Experience.* Lynchburg, Va.: The Rolfing Partnership, 1991.

Wing, Heather. *Rolfing Movement Integration: An Introduction.* Boulder: Rolf Institute.

ORGANIZATIONS

European Head Office
European Rolfing Association
Ohmstrasse 9
80802 Munich, Germany

International Rolf Institute
302 Pearl Street
Boulder, CO 80306

The Rolf Institute
205 Canyon Boulevard
Boulder, CO 80302

The Rosen Method

What and When

The Rosen Method is a system of emotional and physical therapy, including verbal exploration of personal history, physical exercise, and massage for realignment. Usually you are lightly clothed and lying down on a massage table. Try it when you want to explore connections between your physical habits and your emotional history.

Posture and Mobility

Marion Rosen began her training in Munich in 1936 with Dr. Gustav Heyer and his assistants, studying breath and relaxation techniques combined with psychotherapeutic treatment. In Sweden in 1939 she participated in a physical-therapy training course and took her official exam in Stockholm. Rosen came to the U.S. in 1940 to take premedical studies at the University of California, Berkeley. In 1944 she

> I have found that two factors are critical when you work with a person
> suffering from backache. One of these is to develop mobility of the musculature.
> The second is to develop good posture.
>
> —MARION ROSEN

attended the Mayo Clinic's training course in physical therapy and took the National Registry Exam. She worked as a physical therapist at Kaiser Hospital in Richmond, California, until 1946, when she went into private practice.

Gradually Marion Rosen's work became refocused on relaxation techniques, because she "found this approach most effective in the long run." She was on the staff of the Psychosomatic Medicine Clinic in Berkeley and conducted a private practice. Her techniques combine massage, posture education, exercises for limbering body structure through joint flexibility, and breathing techniques. She taught classes for men and women of all ages in several centers in Berkeley, and saw private patients in her office in Oakland.

An Interview with Marion Rosen

The way our bodies are made, we need to move every part at least once in twenty-four hours to retain our mobility. I have developed a series of exercises for the joints. I call it "joint hygiene," because you must move the joints to keep them at their maximum mobility potential. Most people move their whole body in the course of the day, unless they have a sedentary occupation, like psychiatry or office work. Then they sit in one position hours at a time. These people really have to exercise in order to get their bodies working the way they should.

Because of its structure the back is more apt to suffer from disuse and tension. So a lot of my therapy focus is on back movements. The back is structurally prone to problems because we don't walk on all fours anymore. Since we walk upright, one area of the back, around the fourth and fifth lumbar vertebrae, is set at a particularly precarious angle. If that angle gets exaggerated in any way by posture or activity, back troubles often result. It is important that the pelvic and lower-back relationship is at its best. If you lose the balance of the spine, you have to relearn it.

Sometimes I will prescribe a special set of exercises for people, and they recover from their problems. But they may come back five years later and say, "I have back pains again." I ask them, "Did you do the exercises?" They say, "I did them for three years and stopped. Then the pain came back." As long as they kept the spine moving, they could function without pain. Other than posture, mobilization seems to be the most important factor in preventive care.

I define good posture as "the way to carry your body with the least amount of effort." Does the spine really balance itself? Actually, it should need little support from the musculature. The muscles are there to move the bones of the spine, not to hold them.

One never should say, "I will always have a disability." Many things are apt to get better when you allow yourself to move. I have had people with diagnosis of incurable, congenital difficulties. But with proper movement they lost their aches and pains.

The body has an endless longing to improve and to work. If you give the body half a chance, it will get better.

Pleasurable movement is totally different from forced movement. People say, "Should I do this exercise ten times?" I say, "Do it a few times and feel good; then stop." At first you may do it because you have to, but later as you get the feel of it, it becomes pleasurable. And that is when it serves the body.

Anne Kent Rush
—*The Basic Back Book*
Summit / Simon & Schuster

Memories Are Unmade by This

The Rosen Method combines light massage with suggestions for emotional verbal exploration to provide gentle encouragement to release old memories that can cause ill health. Marion Rosen became well known during her physical-therapy practice for her ability to cure psychosomatic disorders. She opened a school in 1977 in Oakland, California, to train others in her method.

Marion Rosen noticed during her career as a physical therapist that the clients who benefited most from her treatments were those who verbalized their related emotions during the sessions. So she formalized her techniques and trained others in her particular combinations of verbal and physical therapy.

A Rosen Session

+ During a Rosen session the client usually lies on a comfortable massage table in his or her underwear and is covered by a light blanket.

+ The therapist emphasizes relaxed, deep breathing to facilitate the release of memories and feelings that may be disturbing the client.

+ The therapist also talks to the client in a noninvasive way to help guide the client through difficult memories.

+ The therapist accompanies the verbal work with gentle massage and body manipulation to release physical tension.

+ Since the sessions may open up traumatic as well as pleasant memories, the client needs to be prepared to enter into a process of serious self-examination. The Rosen Method does not offer psychotherapy in the usual sense, but prefers to pursue gentle self-examination and support.

MARION ROSEN'S FLEXIBILITY MOVEMENTS

Rosen put together a series of movements to loosen up every joint in your body. You need to move the joints in your body or the synovial fluid will dry up, which causes your joints to become tense and tight. Moving them even a tiny bit each day keeps your joints producing this fluid, which keeps the joints flexible.

Exercises

SHOULDER JOG

Begin with the Shoulder Jog. Standing, bend your arms at the elbows, and bring one arm forward while the other goes back. Move at the shoulder as though you were jogging, but move only your arms. Move with your breathing so that you inhale as one arm goes back, and exhale as it comes forward.

STRETCH UP

Raise your arms over your head. Inhale; look at the ceiling; stand up on your toes, and reach with both arms, stretching your fingers as high as you can toward the ceiling so that you open up your rib cage and really stretch your back upward. Exhale and relax.

HITCHHIKE

Stand with your weight on your right leg, and your knees slightly bent. Let your left leg relax. Make a circling hitchhiking motion with your right arm so your shoulder rotates. Repeat this on the other side.

SIDE BENDER

Inhale. Keep your feet about shoulder width apart. Let your arms relax at your sides. Exhale and bend from your waist toward the left. Be sure that you don't lean forward, but to the side over your hip. Bring your right arm slowly up over your head and let it move to the left in a relaxed arc. Let your head and neck relax toward the left also. This will open up that difficult-to-reach area around your rib cage, from your hips to your shoulders. Inhale as you come to the center again. Relax your arms at your sides. Now repeat this exercise with your other arm, leaning toward the right.

WING ROCK

This exercise is similar to the Shoulder Jog. Bend your arms at the elbows; relax your hands loosely. Stand in a comfortable position. This time bring your elbows out to the side, up toward the ceiling. Now raise one elbow higher as you lower the other. You can feel that this motion moves the muscles around your shoulder blade. Check your knees to be sure that they are still gently bent and your legs are comfortable.

HANG LOOSE

Lean forward with your knees bent. Relax your spine and neck and let your arms hang toward the floor. It's important to keep your knees bent so that you don't strain your back. Be sure to let your neck fully relax. You can shake your head a few times to loosen your neck and shoulders. Let your arms hang. This position could be a warm-up for touching your toes. But now you're simply relaxing. Let your arms swing and rotate and feel how this gently opens your upper back around your shoulder blades.

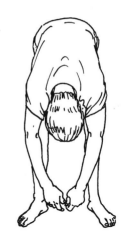

BEND AND STRETCH

Spread your feet wider apart than your shoulders, keeping your pelvis tucked under. Inhale. Spread both arms out to the side. Exhale as you lean to your left and touch your left toe with the fingertips of your right hand. Inhale as you stand up again. Next exhale, lean over, and touch your right toe with the fingertips of your left hand. While you're doing this exercise, make sure your head and neck are relaxed forward, so that you're not straining by holding your head and looking up. You should be looking down at your toes; now touch your toes, helping yourself by bending your knees even more. Gradually the movement will become comfortable so you can do it with your knees just slightly bent.

FINAL REST

Lie down on your back, relaxing your whole body. Notice how you feel as a result of doing these warm-ups and see if your body doesn't feel more alive, more sensitive, and softer.

ℐ BOOKS ℐ

Rosen, Marion, with Sue Brenner. *The Rosen Method of Movement.* Berkeley: North Atlantic Books, 1991.

ℐ ORGANIZATIONS ℐ

Rosen Method Professional Association
825 Bancroft Way
Berkeley, CA 94710

13.

The Rubenfeld Synergy Method®

What and When

Rubenfeld Synergy integrates bodywork, intuition, education and psychotherapy. You are clothed during a session. It is focused on learning through pleasure rather than through pain, and the sessions, employing "listening touch," are gentle, noninvasive, and slow. Particularly helpful to those under great stress.

Bodymind Integration

The integration of body, mind, emotions, and spirit by Ilana Rubenfeld began in the 1960's. She directed body mind energy as if she were conducting a symphony—as well she should, having graduated from the Juilliard School of Music. She conducted until a back spasm and emotional stress reorchestrated her life.

During Rubenfeld's search for relief, she found the Alexander Technique, which used touch to teach her how to use her body more efficiently. However, during her lessons with Judy Leibowitz, she began to express emotions. Judy wouldn't talk about these feelings and referred Rubenfeld to a psychotherapist. He used "talk" to process her emotional state and balked at including touch. Ilana worked with both professionals for many years—appreciating each method—but she yearned to work with one person who could use both talk and touch simultaneously.

She determined to create a system that addressed all aspects—convinced that a person's mind, body, emotions, and spirit function in unison and must be healed together to produce a lasting change.

Joy, Tears, and Laughter in a Rubenfeld Synergy Session

+ Rubenfeld's system is based on her conviction that people heal through a process of transforming suffering to joy.

+ The techniques involved are gentle, noninvasive, supportive, and include humor as a vital element in balanced human functioning.

+ Because the work deals with deep awareness and gradual personal growth, a series of sessions may be appropriate. Certification training is also long, a total of sixteen hundred hours.

+ Client and therapist seek causes of problems and, through gentle touch and verbal exploration, resolution of the issues, and integration of present emotions and actions.

Client and Synergist meet in a sacred healing space.

—ILANA RUBENFELD

The Body Tells the Truth

Ilana Rubenfeld credits six key realizations that changed her life and led her to create the Rubenfeld Synergy Method. She calls these moments of realization her Aha! Experiences.

#1—**You're not always doing what you think.** You may think your body understands one mental message, but then discover you're doing the opposite and feel conflicted.

#2—**Touch is a powerful means of communication.** Sometimes touch is more powerful and clear than words.

#3—**The body is an interconnected system.** Each part affects all parts. Movement demonstrates how body mind components are connected.

#4—**You don't have to know why to have an experience.** Some preverbal, emotional events are not easily expressed in words. Rational explanations may interrupt and weaken an experience. Authentic experience is in your body. Perhaps rational understanding will come later.

#5—**Emotions live in the body.** Memories connected to an experience stay in your body and become part of how you move. "Listening touch" may awaken these emotions and make them available for processing.

#6—**Both talk and touch are needed for people to integrate changes in their physical, emotional, and mental lives.**

Rubenfeld was an orchestra conductor coordinating many parts and this influenced her multilayered work. Rubenfeld Synergy practitioners learn to analyze a session by doing a written map of the work much like a musical score.

Rubenfeld recounts two sessions to illustrate how words and bodies often tell different stories*:

"Lucille, a short, lively woman about seventy-five years old, flew out of her chair and onto the table when I asked for a volunteer. She began to sob and complain about how, after forty years, her husband had left her to find his own 'space.' Slipping my hands under her back, I discovered that it was relaxed, soft, pulsing with energy—'juicy.' I asked her what was going on in her life right now. She looked at me sheepishly and said 'I have two boyfriends.' We both started to laugh. Gasping for air, she exclaimed that her sex life was wonderful and both men showered her with affection and attention. Lucille thought she should be miserable; after all, her husband had left her. Yet her body told a different story, one that didn't agree with what she was saying.

"John, a depressed and sad young man, lay motionless on the table. I tried to gently move his head. It was stuck. When I slipped my hands under his back it felt like a sheet of steel. He explained that his fiancée had left him suddenly and he was confused. I asked him to imagine his fiancée and speak to her.

"In a soft, placating voice he said, 'Joan, I forgive you . . .' As he spoke, his back tightened even more, as if it were saying 'You must be kidding! I'm furious!' His back clearly contradicted what he was saying.

"'If your back had a voice, what would it say?' I asked.

"He began to pound the table, yelling, 'I'm so angry at what you've done!' Even though he thought he should forgive her, his body was expressing his inner emotions.

"After several sessions, he was able to contact and express his grief and sadness. Then, looking and feeling more relieved, he was genuinely ready to forgive her. His body, mind, and emotions were now congruent."

*Stories reprinted with permission of Ilana Rubenfeld from her chapter in *Getting in Touch*, edited by Christina Caldwell, Ph.D.

BOOKS

Forman, Suzanne. "The Rubenfeld Synergy Method® Addresses Mind, Body and Spirit." Massage Therapy Journal, Vol. 71, January/February 1998.

Rubenfeld, Ilana. *"Beginner's Hands: Twenty-five Years of Simple Rubenfeld Synergy—the Birth of a Therapy."* Somatics, Spring/Summer 1988.

"The Listening Hand"; Bantam Books, 2000.

"Ushering in a Century of Integration." *Somatics*, Autumn/Winter 1990–91, pp. 59–63.

Simon, Richard. "Listening Hands." *Family Therapy Networker*, September/October 1997.

ORGANIZATIONS

Canadian Association of Rubenfeld Synergists
112 Lund Street
Richmond Hill, Ontario L4C5V9

Rubenfeld Synergy Center
115 Waverly Place
New York, NY 10011

National Association of Rubenfeld Synergists
1000 River Road (#8H)
Bolman, New Jersey 07719

http:\\members.aol.com\RUBENFELD\SYNERGY\index.html

"Rubenfeld on the Road"; Audiotaped exercises; from The Rubenfeld Synergy Center, New York.

14.

Tellington Ttouch

What and When

Tellington Ttouch is a system of light finger massage of animals to heal injuries from accidents and to reduce stress. Try when a vet is not available in case of emergency or simply when you want to give your pet a relaxing treat.

For All Things Bright and Beautiful

This is bodywork for birds, mammals, and reptiles. They have stress and back problems too.

Linda Tellington-Jones grew up riding horses and mastered a great variety of equine disciplines, winning top awards in every field in which she competed. As an adult her astonishing array of accomplishments continued. Among her numerous achievements are setting records in hundred-mile rides, breeding top Thoroughbreds, training in classic cavalry horsemanship, cofounding the Pacific Coast Equestrian Research Farm, being selected as an American Horse Show Association judge, co-writing a book on physical therapy for the athletic horse, teaching horse psychology at the University of California, conducting clinics in Germany to retrain problem horses, conditioning Olympic-level horses, and expanding her physical-therapy techniques to many other kinds of animals besides horses.

In tests on horses it was discovered that when the Ttouch was applied, the horses generated all four brain patterns: alpha, beta, theta, and delta. Tellington-Jones suspects that Ttouch gets the cells "talking" to each other and "turns on the electrical lights in the body," so that the animal can overcome its instinctive fight, flight, or freeze response and begin to think.

Called "Tellington Ttouch" or "T-Ttouch," Linda's physical training for horses was greatly influenced by her study of the Bodywork of Moshe Feldenkrais. She applied Feldenkrais's gentle, sophisticated movement training to horses and other animals to invent a system for calming, rejuvenating, and improving the performance and spirits of normal and problem animals.

Mickey Hego, ASPCA manager of Companic Animal Services, explains Ttouch is an intimate process that facilitates bonding between people and animals: "It is the opposite of the hostile and adversarial attitude that so often accompanies our dealing with other creatures. Based on the principle that each animal is an individual with feelings and emotions

The work we do is not magic. It is based on the idea that the nervous system is
connected to the brain and that tension, fear, and pain held in the body keep
an animal from functioning fully. The Ttouch cannot replace veterinary medicine, and it
is not a cure for everything. But it can contribute positively toward relieving
a wide variety of behavior and health problems.

—LINDA TELLINGTON-JONES

that must be considered, Ttouch can be a valuable component of teaching people to respect animals and treat them with more consideration. It is a very basic way of communicating."

Exercise

HORSE ROCK-A-BYE

To help your horse relax, try the Neck Rocking. With one hand on the crest and the other on the jugular, gently rock the top and bottom of the horse's long neck back and forth. When done well most horses nearly fall asleep.

Exercise

TO CALM A DOG

Place your cupped hand over the dog's ear. Gently slide your hand from the base of the ear out to the tip. Apply slight hand pressure as you slide so that the inner and outer surfaces of the ear are lightly stroked. Be sure to stroke the tip as you slide off the ear. Use this light motion, as long as is necesssary, on both ears. This will help calm a dog in trauma or shock.

✐   TAPES FROM TTOUCH   ✐

Ttouch
PO Box 1481
La Quinta, CA 92253

Item # DLXDP2 *Ttouch for Dogs*—Deluxe Package $29.95

Item # DLXCP2 *Ttouch for Cats*—Deluxe Package $29.95

Item # DLXHP2 *Ttouch for Horses*—Deluxe Package $29.95

Item # LLAMA *Ttouch for Llamas*—Deluxe Package $29.95

ORGANIZATIONS

American Holistic Veterinary Medical Association
2214 Old Emmorton Road
Bel Air, MD 21015

WEB SITES

AltVetMed—Complementary and Alternative Veterinary Medicine
www.altvetmed.com
Information on treating your pets with several natural approaches.

Therapeutic Touch

What and When

Therapeutic Touch is a system of analyzing your energy field, or aura, for signs of imbalance and then bringing the energy into balance. It is noncontact healing. The practitioner moves his or her hands above your body, while visualizing harmony and health. Usually you are fully clothed and sitting upright in a chair. Try it when the ailing person is too sore to be touched, when other measures fail, or because it feels good to you. Sessions last about half an hour.

Blue Light Special

If you're feeling shy but would like to try some Bodywork, you might start here. In this system your clothes stay on and the healer's hands stay off. Therapeutic Touch is a Western version of several Eastern energy healing systems. Dora Kunz, a spiritual healer, and Dolores Krieger, a registered nurse, worked together to formalize their

Therapeutic Touch   109

techniques of Therapeutic Touch, which attempt to bring a person's energy cycles into balance and calmness. Then the body's self-healing powers can clear up any illness.

The receiver of Therapeutic Touch has a different experience from that in most other therapies because you stay fully dressed and in an upright position, usually seated sideways in a chair to give the practitioner access to your back. The practitioner receives information from the client's body for diagnosis through energy sensations in the palms of the hands. To best receive this subtle energy information, the practitioner mentally calms her own energy by breathing and centering exercises that balance her own fields during the session. Most often the practitioner holds her hands several inches away from the person's body, rarely making physical contact. The name "Therapeutic Touch" refers not to physical contact but to energy contact channeled through the palms.

Hands-Off Healing

+ Therapeutic Touch healing assumes that the human body is not defined completely by its physical body covered with skin, but has a larger perimeter of layers of energy surrounding it. Thus it is not necessary to touch your body. The healer can move his or her hands around your surrounding energy layers.

+ The practitioner visualizes these surrounding layers, or aura, and seeks to restore harmony there.

+ Some people visualize layers of different colors around people and interpret their state by analyzing the symbolic meanings of the colors. Blue is considered to be a positive symbol of deep calm and balance.

Therapeutic Touch Session Format

+ **Center.** The practitioner/healer needs to relax and focus his or her own energy in order to help balance someone else's. Breathing slowly and deeply begins the relaxation. Visualize a peaceful place or event or whatever image is calming to you. The receiver is encouraged to do some centering also to prepare for treatment.

+ **Assess.** Standing in front of the client, the healer kneels and quickly passes her palms, held about six inches away, down the front of the client's body. This quick minute-or-so process is repeated behind

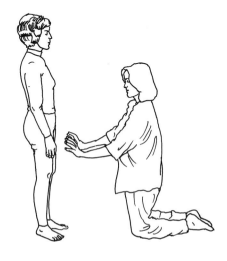

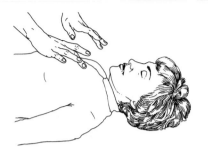

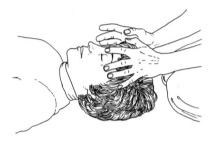

the client. Feeling for clues to energy imbalance, the healer notes areas of cold, hot, pulse, static, colors, or sounds. Each person receives clues through different senses.

+ **Unruffle.** This term refers to the process of smoothing out any blocks in the receiver's energy field. A general calming of the energy can be achieved by a gentle, downward, sweeping motion of the hands, moving from the top of the head down to the feet, but not touching.

+ **Transfer energy.** Placing her hands about four to six inches over the spots on the client's body that feel blocked, the healer directs life energy (not her own—this would tire her) from the air into the client to balance the energy. The Therapeutic Touch practitioner is a channel for universal power. If you are channeling, you can visualize light or heat passing from the atmosphere into yourself, down your arms and hands, and into the client's body.

Exercise

PALM CIRCUIT

Centuries ago healers, martial arts masters, and spiritual teachers felt subtle currents during their practice and included systems for directing them in their exercises to deepen the energizing effects of their movements. Modern technology can locate and measure these electromagnetic currents in the body. Kirlian photographs can sometimes capture them on film. You can do a simple exercise to feel these currents. Try this technique with your hands. Later you can try directing the energy to any part of your, or someone else's, body to revive the energy.

- ◆ Sit comfortably, eyes closed, hands resting palms-up on your knees. Relax any tense muscles you feel by imagining that each time you exhale, a little more tension leaves your body with the breath. Allow your breathing to be low in your body so your belly puffs out a bit as you inhale and sinks back in as you exhale.

- ◆ Now imagine what it would feel like if you could send your exhalation through the center of your body, down your torso, to massage your muscles from the inside. Allow your breath to bring warmth, air, and relaxation to any tight area.

- ◆ As you exhale, imagine you can send air down through your shoulders and arms and eventually into your hands. What would it feel like if you could exhale down your arms and out the center of your palms, through a spot about the size of a small coin?

- ◆ Now raise your palms so they are facing each other at about waist height. As you inhale, oxygen is drawn into your body and is spread through your body with your blood. The increased circulation to your hands as a result of your breathing and your focus sometimes brings a sense of warmth and tingling. The muscle relaxation and improved circulation increase the body's electrical flow between your facing palms.

- ◆ Certain positions also intensify the current. Allow your hands to move slowly in any direction they want. Try holding them different distances apart to see where the energy feels stronger and where it weakens. You may sense a flexible shape to the airspace. Sometimes it feels as though you are holding a ball between your hands. If so, allow your palms to circle the shape.

- ◆ The more you relax and direct your breathing down your arms, the stronger the sensation will become. You will notice that this process releases tension in your shoulders and arms. You can use this directed breathing to relax tight muscles in other parts of your body.

Exercise

HEALING HANDS

Healers train to intensify this electromagnetic current so they can send relaxing sensations to other people. You can place your palms on the person's body. Or you can hold your hands above the body without touching. When you become more skilled in increasing your energy, you can even send it to people far away. You also may experience the exchange of these natural currents between two people. Being able to send and receive this energy gives you a resource for reviving tired muscles and spirits.

- As you breathe, oxygen flows to various parts of your system through your bloodstream. Visualize this process and imagine you can direct the stream of oxygen and electrical energy into your hands and then into a specific body part of the person you want to heal.

- Imagine you can send electrical energy as you exhale down through your arms and into your hands. When you sense some warmth in your palms, let your hands move around the targeted body area, experimenting with how far apart or close to move them for the most intense sensation. Direct energy into any body part (yours or someone else's) you want to heal. You may want to try imagining light is being directed by your hands, to see if this image is more effective for you.

BOOKS/TAPES

Krieger, Dolores, Ph.D., R.N. *Accepting Your Power to Heal: The Personal Practice of Therapeutic Touch.* Sante Fe: Bear & Company, Inc. 1993.

——. *Living the Therapeutic Touch: Healing as a Lifestyle.* New York: Dodd, Mead, 1987.

——. *The Therapeutic Touch: How to Use Your Hands to Help or Heal.* Englewood Cliffs, N.J.: Prentice-Hall, 1979.

——. *The Therapeutic Touch Inner Workbook.* Santa Fe: Bear & Company, 1997. A manual for preparing yourself to be a healer and maintaining focus.

Kunz, Dora. *The Personal Aura.* Wheaton, Ill.: Theosophical Publishing House, 1991.

Macrae, Janet, Ph.D., R.N. *Therapeutic Touch: A Practical Guide.* New York: Alfred A. Knopf, 1992.

Montagu, Ashley, Ph.D. *Touching: The Human Significance of the Skin.* New York: Harper & Row, 1986.

Tape: *The Art of Breath and Relaxation*—Living Arts Catalog—$20.00

ORGANIZATIONS

Center for Human Caring
University of Colorado Health Sciences Center
School of Nursing
4200 East Ninth Avenue, Box C288–8
Denver, CO 80262

Colorado Center for Healing Touch
198 Union Boulevard, Suite 204
Lakewood, CO 80228

Nurse Healers Professional Associates, Inc.
1211 Locust Street
Philadelphia, PA 19107

16.

Trager Psychophysical Integration

What and When

Trager Psychophysical Integration is a system of exercises called "Mentastics", plus extremely gentle therapist manipulation of the limbs of the body designed to align the posture and correct cramping or nerve pinching. You can be nude or clothed. Try it when you need therapy after injury and are too sore to be massaged deeply, or simply for stress reduction or posture realignment.

Lightness of Being

Milton Trager did not seek his talent as a healer, it surprised him. He grew up as a frail child in Chicago in the early 1900s. His family moved to Miami when he was sixteen. To build his strength he began doing gymnastics and running on the beach.

The combination had a meditative, calming effect and later he would title his exercise system "Mentastics."

At eighteen Milton began training to be a professional boxer. In this world he was introduced to sports massage. One day when his trainer looked too exhausted to massage him, Milton offered to switch roles. The trainer's enthusiastic response to Milton's massage encouraged Milton to try his hands on others. Trager's intuitive massage cured his father's sciatica and helped other people in his neighborhood. When a sixteen-year-old polio victim whom Trager massaged walked, Trager stopped boxing to safeguard his hands and expanded his massage exploration.

Because Trager's work was not understood or recognized medically at the time, he had trouble securing a solid professional position. But when he cured a paralyzed girl in a hospital in Guadalajara, the university there established a clinic for him and allowed him to study in their medical school as well as to continue his unique work there for some time. Trager came to Esalen Institute in California in 1973 to demonstrate his work. A teacher there, Betty Fuller, was so impressed that she formed the Trager Institute to train others in this remarkable method. Dr. Trager taught his work throughout the U.S. and Europe. Today there are Trager schools where students can take courses and become certified.

Play Therapy

- ✦ The strongest characteristics of the Trager method are lightness, simplicity, and playfulness.

- ✦ The aim of the work is to impart the physical message to your unconscious that movement can be effortless.

- ✦ To teach by example the Trager practitioner employs very light, easy motions to manipulate your limbs and muscles. These gentle movement patterns send new messages to the recipient's nervous system that cause change in your habitual ways of moving and responding.

+ This newfound ease and pleasure of movement affects the person emotionally also, and reduces stress while opening gentler ways of functioning with others.

Hookup: A Meditative Process of Peaceful Aliveness

+ Trager process is based on the belief that we are surrounded by a force, a life-giving, life-regulating force to which we can connect or "hook up." The first step for going into hookup is to acknowledge that there is a force greater than yourself.

+ The second step for going into hookup is to allow it to happen. Do not try.

+ Trying is an effort, and effort creates tension. Dr. Trager says that to try is to fail.

+ Hookup is the same as meditation. There are many levels. One can go deeper and deeper into relaxation.

+ Deeper beyond meditative relaxation is peace.

+ There is no design. Just spend more time walking about with the knowledge that you are enveloped by this life force that nourishes and supports you.

+ Hookup is not a passive state. It is dynamic, vibrant; yet peaceful. The

Hookup is the most essential element of Mentastics. Through hookup, Mentastics can reach a point of meditative motion as the movements become effortless and rhythmic with a dancelike quality. One can sense and feel a new and desired lightness and agelessness that pleasures the body. One can become intimately aware of one's body as the mind becomes a subtle participant in every movement.

—MILTON TRAGER, M.D.

enemies to relaxed movement are tension, worry, and anxiety. Hookup is allowing your natural movement.

> Dr. Trager says, "Mentastics is a coined expression meaning 'mental gymnastics.' They are mentally directed movements that suggest to the mind feelings of lightness, freedom, openness, grace, and pleasure resulting in an ageless body."

A Typical Mentastics Session

Mentastics are the movement exercises in the Trager system. Trager also includes Bodywork training for practitioners who want to study how to align another person's posture and improve his range and ease of movement. A session lasts about one hour and is priced from $60 to $150. The client, clothed or nude according to preference, lies down on a massage table. The Trager practitioner gently moves, lifts, and lightly shakes the limbs of the client, in a manner similar to the spontaneous light Mentastics Exercises. The practitioner is selecting movements in answer to the classic Trager questions, "What can be freer, lighter, softer, in this movement?" By showing the person that the body part can move with such ease, the practitioner sends a message to the muscles of a relaxed option to tension. You learn to free the body gently of tension and your posture returns to proper alignment.

Through movement Trager Mentastics explore a unique approach to self-development and psychophysical integration. Feeling is the core of Trager Mentastic movements. Who we are is the sum of all feeling experiences, positive and negative, in our lives. Our feeling experiences are stored in our unconscious mind and are not erased.

> During my training with Dr. Trager he would repeat, "You're not working with the body; you are working with the mind." Trager movements invite unconscious patterns into body awareness so that the bodymind can choose to release them.
> —SANDI GEKLER, TRAGER PRACTITIONER

The aging process begins early in life, usually around age ten. The rigidity that you feel as you get older is from the effects of the many adverse experiences that have occurred, and these go into your tissues. The tensions and rigidities causing the aging process are mental, not physical, patterns. Youthfulness is for children, but agelessness is available to us. An ageless body is an open and comfortable body. Mentastics offers a path to this freedom.

Mentastics and exercise goals are not the same. In exercise, one is pursuing increased tone, strength, endurance, or speed with much effort. The goal of Mentastics is to hook up with a meditative state of relaxed awareness. Feelings of freedom, lightness, or softness develop within oneself.

The Mentastics Process

+ When you feel stiffness in your body, do not attack it. Do not try to make it freer. The tighter the body, the lighter the movement must be.

At Work

The softness and ease that you develop through Mentastics can be transferred to other areas of your life. . . . At work, or in any situation where you feel tense, simply recall the feeling of lightness that you experienced in doing Mentastics, and you will come into a state of relaxation to the depth in which you have developed the feeling of relaxation in your mind.

—Milton Trager, M.D.

My students often ask me, "Where is the movement coming from? Is it coming from my shoulder, my arm, or my hand?" I say to them, "It is coming from your mind. And if the movement does not originate from your mind, then you are trying too hard. It is a happening."

—MILTON TRAGER, M.D.

+ If you feel pain, discomfort, or fatigue while doing Mentastics, then allow the movement to become lighter, decrease the range or amount of movement, slow down the tempo of the movement, or stop the movement and rest.

+ Do not analyze. Analyzation is a conscious process. Just feel the weight of the part of the body you are moving. Ask yourself, "How heavy can my arm feel?"

+ Or you can slow the movement down. Moving too fast will also take one out of hookup. Mentastics helps develop patience. Play with the resistance you feel. Take your time. You will be rewarded for your patience.

+ It is important that the Mentastic movements be directed from the mind. Begin by asking "What is lighter? What is freer? What is softer? What is more beautiful?" Ask yourself in an undemanding manner. Expect the answer to come. This process develops the power and potential of your unconscious mind.

+ Mentastic movements are very simple, yet their simplicity is a challenge, a personal exploration toward self-development. You may think, *It can't be this easy. I am barely doing anything physically. And yet, I feel a change.* There are no deliberate movements, no wasted motion. Each small movement, each thought, approaches a feeling of freedom and creates an integration of body and mind.

Exercise

ARM SWING TO RELEASE PAIN
AND TENSION IN THE SHOULDERS

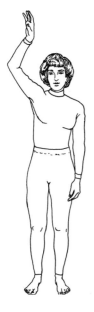

♦ Stand and swing one arm out to the side. Allow momentum to swing the arm up and down. Feel the space you can create in the shoulder and chest as you gently float your arm out to the side. As the arm comes up, the elbow bends at the height of the movement from the weight of the arm.

♦ If you feel tension in any part of your arm or hand, then slow the movement. You cannot feel the subtle trembling in the muscles when moving too fast. Allow the movement to be a soft, steady, rhythmic, quieting motion.

♦ Repeat the arm Mentastics to the other side. An automatic transference of the feeling of lightness will move to the other arm. Recall, "How did it feel to do it on the other side?" Ask, "How can it be moved more softly?"

Exercise

LEG KICK FOR LOWER-BACK
AND KNEE PAINS

♦ Kick each leg once to each side so that you can see and feel your thigh and calf muscles bounce. Keep the foot close to the floor or just barely touching to prevent contraction in the hip. Feel the weight of your leg and the shaking in your calves and ankles. As you kick gently, allow the subtle feeling that your leg is falling down and out of the hip socket.

♦ This movement creates a natural, slight jiggle in the lower back that can relieve general tension. If you can feel this slight bouncing by resting your fingers on the bony structure of the lower back, this indicates a release of tension in the lumbar area. Without the lower-back bounce the kick is worthless for back relief. But do not try to make it bounce.

- Continue to kick while walking as if you are kicking a tin can, with an attitude of indifference, as though you do not care where the can goes. Take small steps. Tension in your thighs indicates you are holding the foot out too long.

- It is never how strong you can kick. Do not shove the legs out or move deliberately. Without plan, let it be rhythmic and expressive, like a dance.

- If you feel tired, stop the movement and rest. If you feel pain, you are using too much effort. Slow down. Allow the movement to originate from your mind by asking, "What is free? What is light? And lighter than that is . . . ?"

- During your day, as you walk, repeat the kicks with a lighter feeling. With every kick you will develop more feeling of softness, which will deepen your feeling of hookup, or relaxed pleasure. For many people with lower-back chronic pain, the Mentastic kick can help them be free from pain.

BOOKS

Juhan, Deane, M.A., *An Introduction to Trager Psychophysical Integration and Mentastics Movement Education.* Mill Valley, Calif.: Trager Institute, 1989.

Trager, Milton, M.D., with Cathy Guadagno, Ph.D. *Trager Mentastics: Movement as a Way to Agelessness.* Barrytown, N.Y.: Station Hill Press, 1987.

The Trager Journal. Mill Valley, Calif.: Trager Institute.

ORGANIZATIONS

Trager Institute
33 Millwood Street
Mill Valley, CA 94941

17.

Zone Therapy and Reflexology

What and When

Zone Therapy and Reflexology are systems of pressure-point massage without oils that focus on finger stimulation of muscles and nerves in the feet. You can be fully clothed, sitting or lying. Try it when you want a general energy pick-me-up or when you want to help heal yourself by working on the spots on your feet that correspond to your health problems.

The Sole of Bodywork

As nonthreatening and soothing as an old-fashioned foot rub, Zone Therapy and Reflexology are pressure-point massage techniques that focus on treatment of the feet in order to improve the general feeling of well-being as well as specific treatment of ailing areas of the body. Elaine Hyams Koelmel, a board-certified Reflexologist in practice over twenty-one years, explains that "Reflexology helps to adjust your body's energy flow in order to keep your organs and glands in a

We can learn how to read and interpret the map of the body
as it is represented in our feet.
—ELAINE HYAMS KOELMEL

constant state of balance...and to aid circulation, body detoxification, and immune, muscular, nerve function."

Reflexology can be used by a trained professional to help cure diseases. But it is also inviting to the beginner because its methods are simple, and the work is focused on a small area, the foot. This is a pleasant place for the new explorer of Bodywork to begin because most people are comfortable with accepting a foot massage while they may be more hesitant to risk a full-body treatment. Bodywork is a journey into the mysteries and marvels of our bodies, and Reflexology is one of the most accessible adventures.

A great number of people have heard about Reflexology, but few know its real history and techniques. Because it is a pressure-point therapy, most assume that Reflexology is an Asian technique, but this is not so. A Connecticut doctor, William Fitzgerald, observed that pains originating in certain organs were associated with seemingly unrelated sore body parts and could be relieved by massage on the head, hands, and feet. Dr. Fitzgerald published a text in 1917 on his work, entitled *Zone Therapy.* Reflexology evolved when Eunice Ingham, a physical therapist, became interested in Zone Therapy. She experimented with points on the foot that correspond with problems in other body parts. As a result of her clinical work Ingham devised a detailed map of the foot, identifying each corresponding organ and body part. Ingham published her findings in 1938 in the booklet *Stories the Feet Can Tell,* which is still on sale today as the primary text for learning Reflexology. Later Ingham founded the International Institute of Reflexology in St. Petersburg, Florida.

It may seem unusual that a technique so similar to aspects of Chinese

For Carl Jung the foot is what confirms Man's direct relationship with the reality
of the earth . . . and a symbol of the soul because it keeps man upright.
—J. E. CIRLOT, *A DICTIONARY OF SYMBOLS*

Acupuncture and Japanese Shiatsu could be developed by a Westerner with no knowledge of these ancient medical systems. But it is also logical that if a healing technique as effective and far reaching as Acupuncture is discovered in one part of the world a similar technique will be discovered elsewhere by those open to understanding how our bodies work, even when the discovery flies in the face of conservative medical thought. It just took Americans a few centuries longer than it did the Chinese to figure out a good pressure-point system. Although Ingham met with much disbelief when she first asserted her ideas on Reflexology, it is today one of the most popular, rapidly growing alternative healing approaches.

Scientific Connections

Reflexology is closely related to Acupuncture and Polarity, but easier to learn and practice. The basic concept behind Reflexology treatment is that, because nerves from the spinal cord and brain eventually thread down the back and legs to the feet, massaging the feet can relay relaxation and improve circulation in other areas of the body. The idea that a point of the foot could be connected to the health of, say, the liver might formerly have been considered pretty silly and unscientific. However, today medical science has developed delicate measuring instruments that can detect very subtle energies previously unknown to us. It is now possible to track Acupuncture- and pressure-point-induced energy currents to confirm their connections.

In the 1970s and -80s neuroscientist Dr. Candace Pert discovered receptors in our cells that take "orders" from roaming information cells on what functions to perform all over the body. From this new theories of body functioning evolved that upset old concepts. They help us see that our body parts are constantly connected by cell messengers. The brain is not the only boss. Dr. Pert's explanation of how messages are carried between seemingly unrelated areas of the body is detailed in her book *Molecules of Emotion* (Scribner, 1997). Because of her work we now have scientific proof of why Bodywork helps us heal and why it feels so good and lifts our spirits. If you have a scientific bent, Pert's writings can explain why Bodywork and Reflexology are so ben-

Basic Reflexology Strokes

Pressure

When first developed, Reflexology was practiced with deep, sometimes painful pressure, but this proved stressful and counterproductive to healing. Happily for us today the procedure has been refined, and now trained practitioners use light to medium pressure and gentle movement. Of course, as in all Bodywork, the receiver has the last word, and pressure should be adjusted to his or her preferences.

Thumb Press

For Reflexology the working area of the thumb is the inside edge of the thumb tip where it would make contact with the surface if your hand were resting, palm-down, on a table or any flat area. Using steady, even pressure, walk the edge of your thumb over the area of the foot on which you're focusing, and move forward by slightly bending and unbending the first joint of the thumb. Leverage this pressure with slight pressure of your four fingers on the other side of the foot.

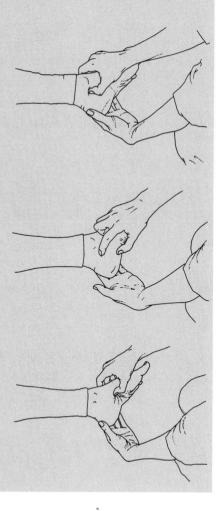

Finger Press

Using whichever finger is strong and comfortable for you, bend the first joint of that finger and massage the area just as you did using the Thumb Press movement.

Push-Up

Use this in a reflex zone when pinpoint accuracy is needed. Bend the first joint of the thumb. Press with the inside corner while your thumb rests on a reflex point. Push in and pull back across the point with your thumb. Do not slide. Stay in contact with the spot and allow your pressure to move only the underlying tissue as you press.

eficial. If you learn by doing and feeling, try getting a Reflexology massage and you'll probably feel so relaxed and content, you won't need more proof.

Exercise

HOW TO BEGIN

+ If you, your friend, or partner is one of the many people who find foot massage relaxing, you can perform the first phase of a typical Reflexology treatment to great effect and with little study. To calm the nerves and relax the patient the first phase of a treatment is normally a massage of the whole sole of the foot.

+ Read the basic Reflexology stroke instructions and perform these strokes carefully all over the soles of both of your feet or both of your partner's feet. Be patient and thorough and your friend will feel very relaxed afterward.

+ If you want to study more details of how to treat specific problem areas, look at the diagrams in *The Massage Book* by George Downing and focus on any spot that corresponds to a sore body part or ailing organ. Spend extra time gently massaging very sore areas.

+ For more information, contact the Foot Reflexology Awareness Association in Mission Hills, California (Phone: [818] 361-0528), as well as the Reflexology Research Center in Albuquerque, New Mexico (Phone: [505] 344-0246).

BOOKS

Bergson, Anika, and Valdimir Tuchak. *Zone Therapy.* Los Angeles: Pinnacle Books, 1974.

Ingham, Eunice D. *The Original Works of Eunice D. Ingham: Stories the Feet Can Tell Thru Reflexology and Stories the Feet Have Told Thru Reflexology* (with revisions by Dwight C. Byers). St. Petersberg, Fla.: Ingham Publishing, Inc., 1984.

Norman, Laura, with Thomas Cowan. *Feet First: A Guide to Foot Reflexology.* New York: Simon & Schuster, 1988.

ORGANIZATIONS

Association of Reflexologists
110 John Silkin Lane
London SE8 5BE
UK

Foot Reflexology Awareness Association
PO Box 7622
Mission Hills, CA 91346

International Institute of Reflexology
PO Box 12642
St. Petersburg, Fla. 33733–2642

Reflexology Association of America
4012 South Rainbow Boulevard
Box K-585
Las Vegas, NV 89103–2059

Reflexology Research
PO Box 35820, Station D
Albuquerque, NM 87176

OTHER PUBLICATIONS/VIDEOS/CDs

Reflexology: The Timeless Art of Self-Healing
    Video with Reflexology chart—60 minutes $25.00

The Reflexology Manual (Softcover—44 pgs.) $17.00
    (Contact International Institute of Reflexology, St. Petersburg, Fla.)

Three

❖

Eastern Bodywork

Introduction

What Is Eastern Bodywork?

Eastern Bodywork is made up of a variety of healing techniques that focus on control of the body's life energy. In Eastern theory we are born with a basic amount of life energy that needs periodic rebalancing and reviving to enable our bodies and minds to function well.

How Is It Different from Western Bodywork?

Western Bodywork looks on your body as a machine in need of repair and manipulation. Eastern Bodywork looks on your body as an energy field in need of constant balancing to function well.

> Most of the energy for the body we get from the air we breathe,
> and not, as is commonly assumed, from food and water.
> —SWAMI VISHNUDEVANANDA, *THE COMPLETE ILLUSTRATED BOOK OF YOGA*

Who Does What Where?

All Eastern Bodywork is based on complex Acupuncture theory. Generally it takes much longer to become certified as a professional than in Western Bodywork. In China traditional Acupuncturists study for about ten years before they are considered fully trained. In the U.S. the training requires about two years. You can practice Acupressure on yourself. In fact, this is highly recommended in Eastern Bodywork as the basis of your preventive health-care regimen.

18.

Acupressure

What and When

Acupressure is a Chinese system using finger pressure on specific points of the skin to stimulate the body's electromagnetic currents to encourage healing. You wear loose clothes or just undergarments and lie down on a therapy table. Try it when you want to relieve specific pains in the body, reduce stress, prevent disease, and revive energy.

A Time-Tested System

The term *Acupuncture* was first proposed as the Western name for the Chinese system by the Dutch physician William Ten Rhyne in the seventeenth century. *Acus* is the Latin word for needle. The layman's name for the system in China is *Cha Zen*, meaning "to stick a needle." Acupressure uses fingers rather than needles to stimulate Acupuncture points and can achieve much the same results.

Before approving a medical treatment today the American Medical Association often tests its reliability for just about ten years. In comparison Acupuncture and Acupressure have proved to be highly effective medical treatments in Asia for over three thousand years. Recently Western doctors have begun giving serious attention to this distinguished record.

Acupressure Basics

+ Acupressure is the massage element of the Acupuncture treatment system.

+ To understand how Acupressure works requires learning about Acupuncture, because they share the same theory.

+ The Acupuncture system identifies specific spots on the body that correlate with the working of various organs and bodily functions.

+ If an Acupuncture point is sore to the touch, this indicates a malfunction of the correlated organ, and treatment to the spot is needed to trigger the body's healing mechanisms.

+ Acupuncture involves inserting thin needles into the spot to stimulate the area. Using exactly the same map of points, Acupressure involves stimulation of the spot simply by finger pressure.

Important Differences
Between the Two

+ Acupuncture is not safe for an untrained person to try. To practice Acupuncture's complex technique demands years of dedicated training.

> What is Acupuncture? Stated most simply, it is a therapy developed by the ancient Chinese that consists of stimulation of designated points on the skin by insertion of needles, application of heat, massage (acupressure), or a combination of these.
> —DR. YOSHIO MANAKA AND DR. IAN URQUHART,
> *THE LAYMAN'S GUIDE TO ACUPUNCTURE*

◆ Acupressure, however, is not only safe for the novice to learn, it is wonderfully helpful to almost anyone for energy revival, stress reduction, and pain relief. Acupressure Massage is a powerful preventive health-care tool available to us all with just a little study.

Almost all other Eastern Body Therapy systems are descendants of Acupuncture and are based on its principles. Although each of the newer systems has something helpful to offer, Acupuncture, including Acupressure Massage, remains the most complete and powerful Asian health treatment system, the granddaddy of them all.

Solving the Energy Crisis

According to ancient Chinese texts, each human body is endowed with a fixed amount of energy at birth, and good health depends on maintenance of this energy level. Daily stresses deplete the life energy (or qi), while food, air, and mental balance replenish life energy. An Acupuncture chart is a map of the lines, called "meridians," along which this life energy flows.

An injury to an area can block the clear flow of energy there and thus cause illness. Proper stimulation of the key points near the blocked area can start the flow of energy again and restore health to the body. Traditionally Acupuncture and

The formal origins of Oriental medicine lie in the philosophy known as Taoism, first developed by Lao Tzu after about 600 B.C. At the core of this philosophy is the belief that human beings are part of nature. This means that we experience the constant flow and change of nature, and it is this flow and change that is reality. Many of us try to create permanence in our lives and in the objects around us, but, because reality is in a state of flux, we should instead try to maintain a state of balance within this constant change. It is this balance that gives us a sense of harmony and well-being, and is the source of our good health.

Acupressure are used on a regular basis to maintain good energy levels in the body for prevention of disease. They can also be used to treat crisis conditions.

To the Point

+ Certain organs respond to Acupuncture and Acupressure much more readily than others. The liver, the spleen, and gall bladder respond extremely well, but

---

Statistics indicate success in ninety percent of cases involving pain, liver disorders, muscle contractures, and heart problems treated by Acupuncture. Cases with bladder involvement show a seventy-four percent ratio of favorable response, and kidney problems a ratio of more than sixty percent.

One significant discovery that has been repeatedly verified by objective measurement is that Acupuncture increases red blood cell (RBC) production. Researchers in both Japan and Europe have found that stimulation of a particular Acupuncture point raises the RBC count of fully matured cells from a minus to a normal level within twenty-four hours. The level is maintained for four to six weeks, at which time the treatment is repeated.

—DRS. MANAKA AND URQUHART, *THE LAYMAN'S GUIDE TO ACUPUNCTURE*

> Every action has an equal and opposite reaction.
>
> —SIR ISAAC NEWTON

other internal organs are more difficult to control, most difficult being the kidneys.

+ Acupressure can relieve pain of all kinds, if there is no lesion, immediately and often permanently.

+ Muscle contractions, even chronic tension, can be relieved.

+ Blood circulation can be improved greatly and hemoglobin production increased, leading to healthier muscle tissue.

+ Sense organ functioning can be improved, even some kinds of deafness.

The Key Is Qi

Energy Balancing is a key part of Acupressure treatments. Life energy, or qi (or chi), can vary within a person in quantity and quality of positive and negative polar charges. To function well the body needs balanced amounts of positive and negative energy currents, similar to the way an electrical battery requires equal amounts of positive and negative charges in order to run. As in electricity the Yin and Yang are not in opposition, but are both required for full-capacity functioning. The Chinese name for positive energy

Chinese medical theory looks for patterns in change, and the Yin/Yang theory was developed to explain these patterns. The terms *Yin* and *Yang* are used to describe the qualities of all things, and their relationships. Everything contains Yin and Yang elements: Yin and Yang are opposite and complementary.

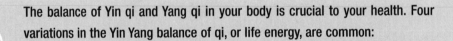

The balance of Yin qi and Yang qi in your body is crucial to your health. Four variations in the Yin Yang balance of qi, or life energy, are common:

1. normal balance and quantity of Yin and Yang qi, which represents health

2. normal Yin qi, but excess Yang qi, which creates heat and overactivity

3. normal Yang qi, but deficient Yin qi, creating heat (especially at night) and a lack of vitality

4. normal Yin qi, but deficient Yang qi, creating lethargy, chilliness, and poor circulation

currents is Yang; the name for negative energy currents is Yin. They cannot exist without each other. Their absence is death. Their tug creates movement, which is life.

Both Sides Now

To Acupuncturists Yin negative and Yang positive energy levels are an index of health, much as a pulse is. The body functions best when the two are balanced equally. Health problems occur when one is low.

Acupressure seeks to address the underlying cause of a physical problem, not just its symptom, by treating the qi energy balance thought to control the body's healing mechanisms. The qi pressure points are places where the meridian energy channels come near the skin's surface so that finger pressure can stimulate them.

A Typical Acupressure Session

+ The only equipment needed for a good Acupressure treatment is a sensitive pair of hands. Be sure your nails are short if you are the practitioner.

- The recipient can be sitting up or lying down. Traditionally the session is given with the client lying on a cotton pad on the floor, but most often in the West the person is lying on a massage table.

- In many Acupressure manuals the client is pictured wearing very little clothing, but this is done mainly to show the position of the hands on the body. In practice it is better for the client to wear thin cotton clothing. The Acupressurist then can concentrate on the feel of the qi energy flow under his or her hands rather than on the texture of the skin. And synthetic fibers disturb qi flow.

- The cost varies from about $50 to $90 per hour.

Exercise

ACUPRESSURE EXERCISE TO STRENGTHEN THE IMMUNE SYSTEM

Use Acupressure and herbs in conjunction with meditation, exercise, Acupuncture, and a healthful diet to strengthen the immune system. The herb Echinacea is thought to strengthen the immune system. Treat points B23, B20, BI3, and St36. To treat means to apply gradual pressure with thumb or finger to the specific Acupressure point as shown on Acupuncture charts. You can work on yourself as well as someone else. Hold each point pressure for about thirty seconds, and longer if comfortable.

CAUTION: Seek professional help if there is weakness, weight loss, continual infection, and depression.

B23, B20, and B13
All these points are two finger widths either side of the spine. The B23 points are level with the second and third lumbar vertebrae. Massage them to stimulate kidney qi—the source of Yin and Yang. Find B20 level with the eleventh and twelfth thoracic vertebrae and tonify to stimulate the spleen—the source of qi and blood. The BI3 points are level with the third and fourth thoracic vertebrae. Press on these to strengthen the lungs.

St36

This point is four finger widths below the kneecap, outside the tibia. Tonify it to strengthen qi and blood circulation to protect the body from infection.

Exercise

POST-VIRAL SYNDROME/ CHRONIC FATIGUE SYNDROME

Symptoms include feeling hot and then cold, headaches, lethargy, dizziness, and pain. In Western medicine the body is viewed as run-down, with a poor response to infection. Chinese medicine sees the problem as illness trapped half in and half out

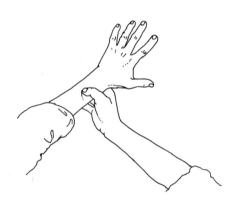

of the body. You need to disperse the trapped qi to the body surface so it can be released. Treat points TH6, GV14, and GB41. Apply gradual thumb or finger pressure to the points and hold for thirty seconds or longer if comfortable.

CAUTION: A complete holistic program is necessary for full treatment of this condition. Seek professional guidance. Acupressure will aid in the healing.

TH6 and GB41

TH6 is four finger widths above the wrist on the back of the forearm. Press on this point to remove stagnation and balance qi in the upper, middle, and lower body. Find GB41 in the furrow between the fourth and fifth toes, just over the tendon on the top of the foot where the bones merge. Massage it vigorously to clear damp heat, hold down rising liver qi, and clear the disease half in and half out of the body.

GV14

GV14 is on the back of the neck, between the seventh cervical and first thoracic vertebrae. Press on this point to clear the Yang channels and regulate temperature.

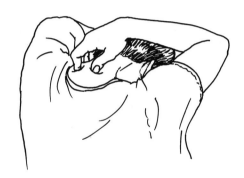

✍ BOOKS ✍

Becker, R. *The Body Electric*, New York: William Morrow, 1985.

Beinfield, Harriet, and Efrem Korngold. *Between Heaven and Earth: A Guide to Traditional Chinese Medicine.* New York: Ballantine Books, 1991.

Blate, Michael. *The Natural Healer's Acupressure Handbook.* New York: Henry Holt, 1977, and Falkynor Books, 1983.

Blofeld, John. *I Ching: The Book of Change.* London: Unwin, 1976.

Chin, Richard. *The Energy Within: The Science Behind Every Oriental Therapy from Acupuncture to Yoga.* Paragon, 1992.

Cline, K. *Chinese Pediatric Massage: Practitioner's Reference Manual.* Portland, Wash.: Institute for Traditional Medicine, 1993.

Hsu, Hong-Yen, and Douglas H. Easer. *For Women Only: Chinese Herbal Formulas.* New Canaan, Conn.: Keats Publishing, 1994.

Kaptchuk, Ted J. *The Web That Has No Weaver.* Chicago: Congdon and Weed, 1983.

Keys, J. D. *Chinese Herbs.* Boston: Charles Tuttle, 1976.

Lu, Henry C. *Chinese System of Food Cures.* New York: Sterling Publishing, 1986.

Mann, F. *Acupuncture: The Ancient Chinese Art of Healing.* London: Heinemann, 1971.

Ni Maoshing. *The Yellow Emperor's Classic of Medicine.* Boston: Shambhala Publications, 1995.

Rush, Anne Kent. *The Modern Book of Massage.* New York: Dell, 1994.

Waley, Arthur. *The Way and Its Power: A Study of the Tao Te Ching and Its Place in Chinese Thought.* New York: Grove Press, 1958.

Wang, C. M., and L. T. Wu. *History of Chinese Medicine.* Taipei: Southern Materials Center, 1977.

Yang, J. M. *Chinese Chigong Massage.* Jamaica Plains, Mass.: Yang's Martial Arts Assoc., 1992.

Zhang, Qingcai, and Y. S. Hong. *AIDS and Chinese Medicine.* New Canaan, Conn.: Keats Publishing, 1994.

ORGANIZATIONS

Academy of Western Acupuncture
112 Conway Road
Colwyn Bay
Chester Springs, PA 19425

Acupuncture Research Institute
313 W. Andrix Street
Monterey Park, CA 91754

Acupressure Institute
1533 Shattuck Ave.
Berkeley, CA 94709

The American Academy of Medical Acupuncture
5820 Wiltshire Boulevard, Suite 500
Los Angeles, CA 90036

American Association of Acupuncture and Oriental Medicine (AAAOM)
National Acupuncture Headquarters
1424 Sixteenth Street, NW, Suite 501
Washington, DC 20036

American Foundation of Traditional Chinese Medicine
505 Beach Street
San Francisco, CA 94133

Association of Chinese Acupuncture
Prospect House
2 Grove Lane
Retford Nottingham DN22 6NA

Australia Acupuncture Ethics and Standards Organization
PO Box 84
Merryland, New South Wales 2160

Chigong Institute
450 Sutter, Suite 916
San Francisco, CA 94108

National Acupuncture and Oriental Medicine Alliance
(The National Alliance)
14637 Starr Road SE
Olalla, WA 98359

Traditional Acupuncture Institute, Inc.
The American City Building, Suite 100
Columbia, MD 21044

WEB SITES

Institute for Traditional Acupressure
www.europa.com/-itm
Information focusing on Chinese herbal medicine, but provides information on the
 Ayurvedic, Tibetan, Native American, and Thai traditions as well.

19.

Reiki

What and When

Reiki is a system of spiritual healing by energy focus. You remain clothed while the practitioner either passes his hands above your body or lightly touches you. Energy also can be sent to sick people far away. The system can only be fully learned from direct instruction by a certified Reiki master teacher. It can be useful when you are too sore to be touched or when you need long-distance healing.

The Life-Force Channel

Mikao Usui was president and minister of the Christian School in Kyoto, Japan, in the mid–eighteen hundreds. One day his student ministers asked him to teach them not only scripture, but also how to carry out the Christian instruction to "heal the sick." Dr. Mikao Usui could not answer this question. He decided to travel to the United States in order to learn how Christian healing was done.

He enrolled in the University of Chicago theological seminary where he completed his doctorate in theology. He corresponded with numerous Christian bishops and leaders about how to heal the sick. Their answers were always "We send the sick to doctors. We only work with the spirit."

In Your Own Backyard

In comparative religion studies at the University of Chicago, Buddhist texts were assigned, and Mikao Usui decided to return to Japan to investigate whether Buddhist records still contained instructions on healing the sick. Dr. Usui interviewed many Buddhist monks and finally found one in Kyoto who agreed to help him learn to heal. Usui spent three years in a monastery reading Buddhist texts called "sutras." Next he determined to learn Chinese in order to look for answers in ancient Chinese manuscripts. And then he learned Sanskrit in order to read the sutras in their original form. At last, here in the most ancient Sanskrit texts from the earliest roots of Buddhism, he found clues to healing.

Dr. Usui was counseled by his Buddhist teacher to meditate in the mountains in order to clear his mind to receive the information. At the end of the twenty-one days Usui had a vision that contained Sanskrit instructions on how to heal the sick. During his long walk down the mountain home he found that he could now heal people's illnesses by laying his hands on them.

Dr. Usui decided to use his new power by living among the beggars in the city and healing them so that they could become more responsible members of society. After healing among the beggars for seven years, Usui found that when he worked for free, the beggars gained physical health, but they remained spiritually broken and could not change their lives. So Usui decided that to heal fully, people need to show initiative and make an effort and conscious decision, so as to become emotionally changed also. It was then that he decided that Reiki treatments should not be free. Reiki practitioners must charge for their services to motivate the receiver to heal. Dr. Usui traveled across Japan training Reiki practitioners and teaching Reiki principles.

Reiki is a Japanese word meaning "universal life energy." Reiki practitioners believe that everyone is born with this energy and that we can learn to channel it through our hands to heal others.

Reiki is different from some other forms of natural healing, such as Intuitive Energy Healing, because the teachers believe that it cannot be taught as most forms are. Reiki can only be transmitted through meditation and through the touch of a Reiki master. People can learn some aspects of Reiki practice, but the full knowledge and power can only be given to a student directly by a master.

Reiki is based on the idea that there is a life-force energy throughout the universe that is available to anyone who knows how to tap it. Through special training people can learn to harness the life energy around them and direct it toward others. The Reiki practitioner then becomes a healing channel for life energy.

We Are Born with It

Reiki Certification

+ **First-degree training:** Four sessions of two and a half hours each, in which a twenty percent power transfer is given by the teacher and "sealed" in the student. Basic Reiki principles and methods for treating ailments are taught.

+ **Second-degree training:** A full hundred percent power transfer, usually administered ninety days after first-degree certification. This allows you to accelerate treatment time; deal with a client's mental and emotional problems; and apply a method for absent healing.

+ **Third-degree training:** The master level. This means the person can teach Reiki and confer first- and second-degree training through power transfers. Master level can be granted only by a grand master who has received Reiki keys rediscovered by Dr. Usui, and to a person who is dedicated to teaching the Usui System of Natural Healing.

The more the therapist uses Reiki, the stronger the healing energy becomes. Reiki will never leave once sealed by a master in the student, unless he attempts to misrepresent the process by claiming to give power transfers without the knowledge that comes with master certification.

I did a lot of meditating. And it came to me that we are more than a channel. Once the students receive the power transfer, we *are* Reiki. We *are* universal life energy. It's the God within us that does the powerful works. Not the ego I Am. But the God I Am; the Reiki, the universal life energy. And that's what we are made of. So without us the healing could not take place. So you're more than a channel. You're a channel, yes, but you are more than that. *Without you the healing could not take place.* You have to love, love enough and care enough to reach out and touch—to place your hands on another—to make anything happen.

—REIKI MASTER VIRGINIA W. SAMDAH

Choosing Whom to Treat

- First, treat yourself.

- Next, treat family members. Normally the family will have provided you with many benefits. Transmitting the health of Reiki is a wonderful way to complete the exchange. Then, consider treating anyone who asks.

- Asking for healing is important. Reiki is a system based on intent. The prospective client should express intent for health by requesting the treatment. Never feel obligated to heal someone if you are too tired or if you are uncomfortable working with him. There must be an energy exchange with the client in the form of payment for your work in order to balance the life energy. You can use money or barter.

- Don't forget pets, animals, and plants either. They have universal life energy and need help too.

Universal Donor

To some Reiki may sound a bit farfetched, but actually its theory is much the same as that of most of the other healing systems based on Eastern philosophy. The concept that there is an all-pervasive life energy that can heal is common to the more mechanical systems from Acupuncture to Zen Shiatsu. Reiki theorizes that the energy healing can occur simply by energy contact with someone who is balanced, without the need for moving the limbs or more complex maneuvers. The unique requirement is training from a Reiki master.

Never diagnose or prescribe. Simply state what you would do
if you had the conditions perceived.

—*THE REIKI HANDBOOK*

A Typical Reiki Session

- Preferably the client lies down on a massage table or a cot to allow gravity to aid the flow of Reiki down into the body. A pillow rests under the head and another under the knees to release pressure in the lower back. A sheet covers the person if chilly. He is dressed in very loose, comfortable clothing. The room should be quiet and ideally used only for treatments because the space will accumulate Reiki charge.

- Most Reiki treatments include the practitioner laying her hands lightly on the client's body. However, if the person's skin is sore or he prefers noncontact, the practitioner moves her hands about an inch over the body.

Exercise

ENERGY HEALING

Reiki treatments resemble the simple laying on of hands known in many worldwide spiritual traditions. The practitioner places his or her palms on a person's body and moves in a sequence of about twenty positions to contact the major energy centers of the physical as well as the emotional aspects of the body. But general healing can be done by hand contact anywhere on the body. The Reiki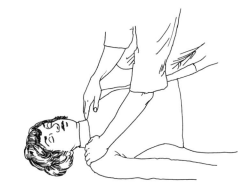

practitioner conceptualizes that life energy is flowing through his or her hands and concentrating in the body of the recipient. The energy will balance any weaknesses in the ill person and restore the body's functioning to health.

+ Be sure the client's feet are not crossed. Otherwise the energy flow will be blocked. The basic rule of Reiki patterns is to treat the front of the body, the head, the back, and to hold in both hands any area that hurts. From eight to ten minutes will be spent on each specific area, and longer for a diseased area. The time is at the intuitive discretion of the Reiki practitioner.

+ The practitioner keeps his fingers together while transmitting energy to focus the flow. The hands are relaxed in order to curve around the body's contours.

+ If a client has a limb or organ missing, the practitioner treats it as though it is present, in order to balance the missing energy. The whole body is treated by laying on of hands, even if the problem is only in one spot, because the body functions as a whole and each area affects all areas.

Exercise

TEAM TREATMENTS

+ More than one practitioner can work with a client to increase the energy flow. Apply hands of one practitioner to the head of the body at the

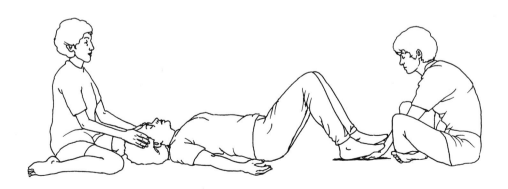

same time that the other practitioner applies her hands to the feet of the body.

◆ One healer can hold the head while the other works on the torso. Or one healer can hold the soles of the client's feet while the other works elsewhere on the body.

◆ Sometimes emotions are released during treatment. The practitioner reassures the client that this is normal and calms the emotions with the energy balancing.

Exercise

REIKI FINISH

◆ The client lies on his or her stomach. Lift the shirt to expose the back.

◆ Use this technique for each leg: Bend the leg at the knee and hold the foot to rotate the toes clockwise, then counterclockwise. Next massage the entire foot. Pinch the Achilles tendon several times. Holding the leg at the ankle, shake the foot a bit. Then gently place it on the table. Stroke each leg from ankle to knee to top of thigh.

◆ The practitioner stands beside the client's hip and reaches across to knead the side between the hip and the armpit with both hands. Then the area is stroked up and down several times. This is repeated on the other side when the practitioner moves around to the far side of the table.

◆ Next firmly massage in a kneading motion the shoulder muscles and base of the neck. Then, sliding from the base of the spine to the neck, rub the flat edge of your thumbs along either side of the spine.

◆ Then drag one finger on either side of the spine: from the neck to the tailbone if the client has no diabetic tendencies; otherwise drag the fingers up from tailbone to the neck. Slide the heels of your hands, fingers touching, from the sacrum up to the shoulders and then down both the person's sides. Repeat several times.

- The client then sits up slowly, supported by the practitioner if the client is at all dizzy. The client sits quietly several minutes before standing.

- The client is told that if he or she feels worse after one treatment, three more treatments will be needed to complete the energy balancing. Usually the client feels better after even one treatment.

BOOKS

Bginski, Bodo J., and Shalila Sharomon. *Reiki: Universal Life Energy.* Trans. Christopher Baker and Judith Harrison. Mendocino, Calif.: LifeRhythm, 1988.

Burack, Marsha. *Reiki: Hands-On Healing for Yourself and Others.* Encinitas, Calif.: Reiki Healing, 1992.

Gleisner, Earlene. *Reiki in Everyday Living: How Universal Energy Is a Natural Part of Life.* WFP, 1992.

Hawayo, Takata. *Living Reiki: Takata's Teaching.* Medocino, Calif.: LifeRhythm, 1992.

Rosenstiel, Leonie, Ph.D. *Reiki: First Degree Manual* (Rainbow Empowerment Series). New York: Dayspring Resources, 1991.

——, *Reiki: Second Degree Manual* (Rainbow Empowerment Series). New York: Dayspring Resources, 1991.

Verheijden, Bernard. "Reiki: The Healing Touch." *Massage,* Issue 50, July/August 1994, pp. 84–89.

Wetzel, Wendy S., M.S.N., R.N. "Reiki Healing: A Physiological Perspective." *Journal of Holistic Nursing.* Vol. 7, No. 1, 1989, pp. 47–54.

ORGANIZATIONS

American International Reiki Association, Inc.
2210 Wilshire Boulevard, Suite 831
Santa Monica, CA 90403

Reiki Alliance
PO Box 41
Cataldo, ID 83810

Reiki: Healing Hands Tel: (800) 254-8464 $15.98

Reiki—Healing Yourself Tel: (800) 254-8464 $22.98
(From Healing Arts Catalog or contact Reiki Alliance.)

20.

Shiatsu

What and When

Shiatsu is an energetic Japanese pressure-point massage system done without oil, as you are lying down (nude or partly clothed) on a mat on the floor or on a low Bodywork table. It can be temporarily painful if the muscle point being pressed is sore. Try it if you need relief from sports strains or enjoy deep, brisk massage.

Finger Pointing to Health

In this system it's polite to point and it feels good too. Shiatsu, a pressure-point massage therapy developed in Japan, has its ancient beginnings in the theories of Chinese Acupuncture, and is similar to Acupressure Massage. What feels unique when you are receiving Shiatsu is the sequence of the pressure points, the relative roughness of the application, and the addition of twists, lifts, stretches, and snaps of different body parts during the treatment. For the practitioner it is a more athletic experience than most other massages.

You should be ready for a bit of a workout if you choose Shiatsu Massage, but done well, Shiatsu is very relaxing and can release muscle cramps and improve energy and circulation.

The Point of Shiatsu

+ The Shiatsu practitioner uses his or her fingertips and thumbs to stimulate acupuncture points and to balance the body's energy.

+ Although a good Shiatsu treatment can be accomplished with the receiver resting on a massage table, in Japan you would be lying on a padded futon mat on the floor while the masseuse or masseur moves around you, applying pressure to various places with the fingers or even elbows and knees. Some Shiatsu practitioners are adept at walking on your back muscles.

+ You stay clothed during this treatment, unless you are in a Japanese bathhouse and are lucky enough to have had a hot tub and back-brush scrub prior to the massage.

+ Currently there is no nationally recognized U.S. certification or licensing for Shiatsu therapists, so when selecting a practitioner seek a recommendation

After World War II, in the years when General Douglas MacArthur was stationed in Japan, he banned as unscientific the practice of most traditional Oriental healing arts. Shiatsu was nearly exterminated. In Japan massage had been performed by the blind, whose touch was deemed especially sensitive. The Japanese Blind Association requested help from Helen Keller. She contacted President Truman, who lifted the ban.

from a trusted health professional. Japanese-trained practitioners may use some different techniques than American-trained practitioners.

Exercise

LEG STRETCH

The receiver lies on the mat on his or her stomach with the knees bent. The practitioner kneels at her right, resting his right hand on the tops of the feet and the left palm on the receiver's sacrum.

To stretch the leg and lower-back muscles, the practitioner applies gradual downward pressure on the sacrum. At the same time the feet and shins are pressed down toward the buttocks. The practitioner works within the comfort zone of the receiver.

Exercise

THE LOWER BACK: SHIATSU ON THE SACRUM

Though the complete Shiatsu system requires training, you can use a simple version of pressure-point massage for very relaxing effects.

- ◆ Stand beside your partner's hips. Lean your weight on your arms as you press your thumbs down on either side of your partner's sacral vertebrae.
- ◆ Gradually angle your weight deeper into your hands so that your thumbs are pressing down into the muscles on the sacrum.
- ◆ When you want to release the pressure, do it just as gradually as you applied it, so that your hands ease out of your partner's muscles very slowly.

> In Japan we call Shiatsu the echo of life. . . . The receiver becomes the
> giver and the giver becomes the receiver as their breathing
> becomes one. . . . I believe touch communication is love.
>
> WATARU OHASHI, DEVELOPER OF OHASHIATSU

+ Then move your thumbs down to the next sacral vertebrae. Gradually apply the pressure of your body weight again.

+ Work your way from the top of the sacrum to the coccyx tip.

+ Then apply the same type of gradual pressure to the lower outsides of the sacrum, from your partner's waist down to the tailbone.

+ The pressure should not be painful to your friend in any way. If it is painful, it means you are either pressing too quickly or too hard for her to relax with the pressure. You might not be in quite the right spot, so shift your position and try another spot.

+ Remember that you'll be more comfortable if you use your body weight to lean and exert the pressure, rather than pushing with your arms. This way you should be able to get a great deal of pressure without straining.

Exercise

THE NECK: SHIATSU POINTS

Place your thumbs on both sides of the cervical vertebrae at the base of the skull on the muscles that go from the occipital ridge down to the base of the neck as it

enters the shoulders. Apply gradual pressure along the muscles. Give this treatment special attention and slow, gentle pressure.

Your partner should angle her head in a comfortable position. Try having your partner rest her forehead on a pillow so that as you press down you won't press her nose into the table. Resting the head on either side may also be relaxing. Even more comfortable can be doing the stroke with the receiver on his or her back so that the giver is pressing upward with the fingers under the neck.

Quick Release

For yourself or for a friend, for quick relief of minor ailments, try pressing on these spots for about seven seconds:

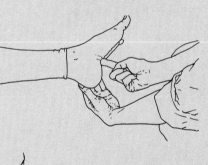

To increase energy—

+ the middle of the palm of each hand

+ on the bottom of the foot in the middle just below the ball of the foot

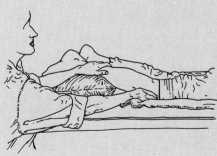

To soothe sore legs—

+ about three inches below each knee in the indentation to the outside of the shinbone

To lower appetite—

✦ centered between the upper lip and the nose

To relieve the common cold—

✦ squeeze the fleshy web between the thumb and fore-
finger near where the web V comes together at the
hand

BOOKS

Bienfield, Harriet, L.Ac., and Efrem Korngold, L.Ac., O.M.D. *Between Heaven and Earth: A Guide to Chinese Medicine.* New York: Ballantine Books, 1991.

Hashimoto, Keizo, M.D., with Kawakami Yoshiaki, M.D. *Sotai: Balance and Health Through Natural Movement.* Tokyo: Japan Publications, Inc., 1983.

Masunaga, Shizuto, with Wataru Ohashi. *Zen Shiatsu: How to Harmonize Yin and Yang for Better Health.* New York: Japan Publications, Inc., 1977.

Namikoshi, Toru. *Shiatsu Therapy: Theory and Practice.* New York: Japan Publications, Inc., 1974.

Ohashi, Wataru. *Do-It-Yourself Shiatsu: How to Perform the Ancient Japanese art of "Acupuncture Without Needles."* New York: E. P. Dutton, 1976.

ORGANIZATIONS

The American Oriental Bodywork Therapy Association
6801 Jericho Turnpike
Syosset, NJ 11791–4413

Shiatsu Society
31 Pullman Lane
Godalming, Surrey, England GU7 1XY

Ohashi Institute
Kinderhook, New York 12106
Fax: (518) 758-6809

VIDEOS

The Art of Pressure	$20.00
Shiatsu for Women	$17.00

(Healing Arts Catalog or contact American Oriental Bodywork Therapy Association.)

Thai Massage

21.

What and When

Thai Massage is a relatively energetic, sometimes rough system for muscle-cramp relief by lifting, stretching, and moving of the client's limbs. No oil is used and you remain clothed as you lie on a floor mat. Try it if you are limber to begin with but want to have your muscles stretched and your circulation stimulated.

Stretch Me; Rock Me

If you've ever wished someone else could do your exercise for you, here's the answer. Traditional Thai Bodywork involves the passive limbs of the client being lifted, stretched, tilted, pummeled, and turned by an athletic practitioner bracing your legs and arms against his or her body. You lie on a floor mat and are dressed in loose clothing.

If traveling through Thailand, you might want to begin your initiation into Thai

Bodywork in the northern part of the country, because the southern region's massage system is much faster and rougher than the northern style and sometimes painful. Northern Thai Massage is identified with Chiang Mai, and Southern Thai Massage is identified with Bangkok.

Thai Massage conceptualizes energy moving through the body in many conduit lines called "sen." Luckily for the beginning student, only ten of the seventy-two thousand sen are considered major. Genuine traditional Thai Massage is aimed at relief of mild to serious medical problems and takes about ten years to study fully. However, less exacting forms are taught and are used for general muscle relaxation and energy balancing.

Exercise

FOOT-PRESS TECHNIQUE

You can use different parts of your bare foot to massage thickly muscled areas. On large curved parts, such as thighs, use your arch to press around the muscle.

On thick, muscular areas, such as the buttocks and backs of the upper thighs, use

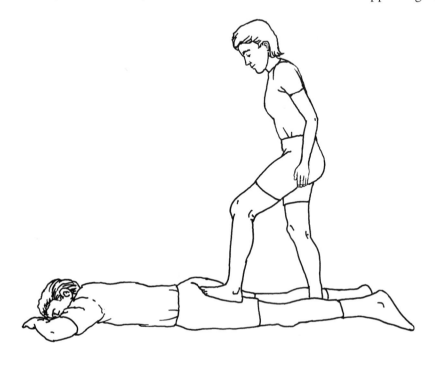

your heel or the ball of your foot. The recipient is lying on a mat on the floor in loose clothing. The practitioner stands to his side and rhythmically leans her body weight down into the muscle; then leans back to release the pressure. Create a gradual, deep pressure and release in a steady pace that is comfortable for both of you.

You can also use the Foot-Press Technique while you are kneeling. One example is to massage the calf muscle with the heel of your right foot while your weight is resting on your left knee. You can regulate your downward pressure by supporting yourself with your hands on the ground.

Exercise

LEG STRETCH

Try this stretch. The receiver lies on her back, arms to the sides, one knee bent while the other leg is straight. The practitioner sits outside the straight leg with his heel placed on the receiver's calf muscle at the crook of her bent knee. From this angle you

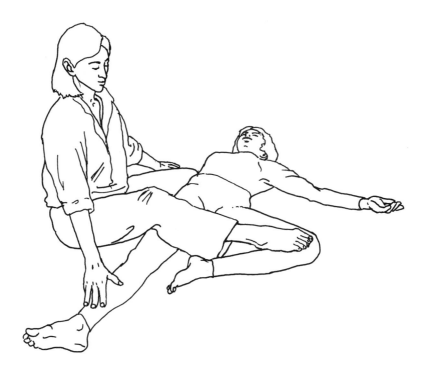

can push the bent leg away from you as you sit to give the receiver's thigh and knee area muscles a pleasant stretch.

HIP ROTATIONS

+ The recipient is lying on his back on a mat on the floor. You stand at the feet and grasp the ankles. You raise both legs and bend the knees, but the receiver's hips and back will be still resting on the ground. Give your partner a chance to relax in this position.

+ Move your palms to the knees and lean your body weight over the legs a bit so you have a firm hold. Then move both legs to one side (right). Next move the legs to the other side (left). Rock the knees from side to side. This will loosen the hip joints, relax the thighs, and help lengthen and straighten the muscles of the lower back.

+ Now add the relaxing Thigh Shake. Hold the ankles. Step back slowly to extend and straighten the receiver's legs.

+ Then shake both legs up and down together. The receiver needs to keep his muscles loose. The giver needs to keep her knees bent to protect her own back from strain.

HEAD-TO-KNEE FOLD

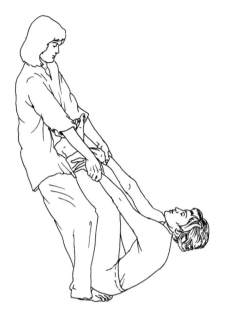

- The receiver lies on his back. Standing up straight, lift and place the receiver's legs along yours so that his feet are near your waist, his knees rest over yours, and his thighs are placed along your shins.

- Then bend over to grasp your partner's wrists. Lean your weight back and stand up straight again, lifting your partner's torso as you do. Ask your partner to relax as you draw his torso toward his legs. Go only as far as is comfortable.

- Then lower the torso very slowly to the ground.

- Next hold your partner's feet and lower the legs to the ground. This stretch can ease sciatic pain, and improve shoulder and hip mobility.

Exercise

CROSSED FEET

This movement increases flexibility in the ankles, arches, and toes, relaxing the tarsometatarsal joints along the ball of the foot.

- Kneel at your partner's feet. With your partner lying on her back, draw the feet together and cross one arch over the top of the other foot.

- Place the palm of your right hand on top of the crossed feet just below the toes. Place your left palm on top of your right hand.

- Lean your weight gradually down on your hands so that the arches are curved more and the toes are pressed down.

- Next release the pressure, cross the feet with the opposite one on top, and reapply your palm pressure.

BOOKS

Mercati, Maria. *Thai Massage Manual.* New York: Sterling Publishing Co., 1998.

VIDEOS

Thai Massage, by Maria Mercati

Bodyharmonics Centre
54 Flecker's Drive
Hatherley, Cheltenham GF516BD
UK

❖

Four

East/West

Bodywork

Introduction

What Is East/West Bodywork?

East/West Bodywork is based on systems that emphasize both energy balancing and body manipulation. The large role of energy balancing in these techniques is the influence of Eastern philosophies and treatments.

How Is East/West Bodywork Different from Either on Its Own?

Coordinating the body manipulation and emotional counseling of the Western techniques with the energy revival of the Eastern techniques results in a pow-

> The body is a multilingual being.
> —CLARISSA PINKOLA ESTÉS

erful, balanced system. You can bring the basic best of both worlds into your daily life.

Who Does What Where?

In the U.S. combining Eastern healing techniques with Western ones began on the West Coast, where large Asian populations make Acupuncture, Acupressure, and Shiatsu available to everyone. Professional organizations for the various techniques can offer therapist referrals. Today many Western doctors study Acupuncture and Acupressure.

22.

Intuitive Energy Healing

What and When

Intuitive Energy Healing is a system of diagnosing physical illness by understanding Indian chakra energy patterns and others and learning to recognize which emotional blocks correspond to which physical ailments. Usually you are fully clothed. It can be particularly helpful when you feel your physical problems are increased by emotional stress.

Nothing but Network

It turns out that molecules have feelings too. We can read all about how Dr. Candace Pert discovered the vital function of our microcosmic melodramas in her book, *Molecules of Emotion* (Scribner). The book that took this scientific information out of the lab and into practical application in our everyday lives is *Anatomy of the Spirit*, by Dr. Caroline Myss, Ph.D. (Three Rivers Press).

No one has captured the breadth and depth of our electromagnetic spiritual framework as well as Caroline Myss. . . . Herein lies the foundation for medicine in the twenty-first century.

—C. NORMAN SHEALY, M.D.

NEUROSURGEON, FOUNDER OF THE AMERICAN HOLISTIC MEDICAL ASSOCIATION

Caroline Myss, Ph.D., has written several groundbreaking books on her work as a Medical Intuitive diagnostician and on her theory that the human structure is based on energy fields, not matter. Dr. Myss views our bodies not as biological machines, but as networks of energy centers (called "chakras" in Indian disciplines) where matter, spirit, and power combine to manifest our selves. Dr. Myss recommends that each of us practice intuitively diagnosing our own imbalances in order to increase our personal power and to catch any disease imbalances early, in time to begin healing them. Part of this process is the cultivation of the skill of symbolic intuition, as well as an impersonal viewpoint.

In *Anatomy of the Spirit* Dr. Myss describes her awakening to her own spiritual diagnostic powers. She explains her model of the body's seven centers of physical/spiritual power. This model is based on a synthesis of teaching from three spiritual traditions—Hindu, Christian, and Jewish—to outline the seven stages of development through which we all must pass in our search for conscious spiritual maturity and balanced functioning.

Chakra Meditation

Western biology calls our body's major nerve junctures "plexuses." The word for a biological nerve plexus in Indian yoga terminology is *chakra*. Each nerve center is thought to be a junction for spiritual as well as physical energy. Mental and physical perceptions attributed to each plexus correspond to its biological functions. All chakras need to be functioning well for the body and mind to be in balance.

A basic chakra meditation is to focus first on the center at the base of the spine, and

> Becoming conscious means changing the rules by which we live and
> the beliefs we maintain. Our memories and attitudes are literally rules that
> determine the quality of life as well as the strength of our bonds
> with others. Always, a shift in awareness includes a period of isolation and
> loneliness as one gets accustomed to the new level of truth. And then
> always, new companions are found. No one is left alone for long.
>
> —DR. CAROLINE MYSS, *ANATOMY OF THE SPIRIT*

then relax each higher area (and its associated function) in sequence. In advanced meditation you can combine breathing and chanting with meditation. This can move the physical spinal, or Kundalini, energy from the base of the spine up to the top of the head.

Be thorough. Partial movement of Kundalini energy produces partial perception and stunted awareness. All the centers must be awakened and connected to produce full spiritual understanding and action. This gradual process can take years while the state of mental union comes and goes. A person who maintains a constant state of spiritual balance is considered enlightened. Most of us see the light only briefly, but even glimpses of clarity can warm a life.

Chakra Centers

1. **Base of Spine, Kundalini Chakra.** Starting point of the body's life energy, seat of basic molecular health and balance.

2. **Pelvic Plexus: Sexual Chakra.** Origin of erotic passion and biological creation.

3. **Solar Plexus: Action Chakra.** Center point of physical and spiritual balance; sense of self and inner calm.

4. **Cardiac Plexus: Heart Chakra.** Diaphragm, center of compassion; can infuse all other chakras with this aspect.

5. **Vagus Nerve and Cervical Ganglion: Throat Chakra.** Communication.

6. **Pineal Gland: Mental Chakra.** Third Eye, center of clear, rational perception; wisdom.

7. **Pituitary Gland: Spiritual Chakra.** Top of head; sense of perspective and unity; symbolized by the Thousand Petaled Lotus.

Developing the Impersonal Mind and Symbolic Sight for Health Diagnosis

+ Develop a practice of introspection, and work to become conscious of what you believe and why. Meditation is a basic tool.

+ Keep an open mind, and learn to become aware when your mind is "shutting down."

+ Recognize defensiveness as an attempt to keep new insights from entering your mental field.

+ Interpret all situations and relationships as having a symbolic importance, even if you cannot immediately understand what it is.

+ Become open to receiving guidance and insight through your dreams.

+ Work toward releasing any thoughts that promote self-pity or anger, or that blame another person for anything that has happened to you.

+ Practice detachment. Make decisions based upon the wisest assessment you can in the immediate moment, rather than working to create a specific outcome.

Chakra Diagnosis by Dr. Myss

A complete energy evaluation has to include all seven chakras, regardless of the location of a physical illness, as well as all aspects of the patient's life. The issues involved in chakras one, two, and three are the ones where most people spend their energy. Not coincidentally, most illnesses result from a loss of energy from these three chakras. Even when an illness, like a heart condition or breast cancer, develops in the upper region of the body, its energy origin can usually be traced to stress patterns in issues of the lower three chakras, such as in marriage or partnership, family, or occupation. Emotions such as rage and anger hit us physically below the belt, while an emotion like unexpressed sadness is associated with disease above the belt. For instance, the major emotion behind breast lumps and breast cancer is hurt, sorrow, and unfinished emotional business generally related to nurturance.

Nurturance also has to do with the health of relationships, however, and relationships are primarily a first- and second-chakra issue. Thus, several—if not all—the chakras have to be used to understand completely why a person has become ill.

For all of the many complex energies that run through our systems, the first chakra is by far the most complex, because it is the beginning or root energy center of your body.

+ Refrain from all judgments—not just those rendered against people and situations, but those that concern the size or importance of tasks. Rather, remind yourself continually of the higher truth that you cannot possibly see all the facts or details of any situation, nor visualize the long-term consequences of your actions.

+ Learn to recognize when you are being influenced by a fear pattern. Immediately detach from that fear by observing its influence on your mind and emotions; then make choices that weaken the influence of those fears.

+ Detach from all values that support the belief that success in life means achieving certain goals. Instead, view a successful life as a process of achieving self-control and the capacity to work through the challenges life brings you. Visualize success as an energy force rather than a physical one.

- Act on your inner guidance, and give up your need for "proof" that your inner guidance is authentic. The more you ask for proof, the less likely you are to receive any.
- Keep all your attention in the present moment—refrain from focusing on the past or worrying about the future. Learn to trust what you cannot see far more than what you can see.

BOOKS

Myss, Caroline, ANATOMY OF THE SPIRIT: The Seven Stages of Power & Healing. New York: Harmony, 1996.

Myss, Caroline, WHY PEOPLE DON'T HEAL AND HOW THEY CAN. New York: Harmony, 1997.

Myss, Carolyn, Ph.D., *Anatomy of the Spirit*. New York: Three Rivers Press, 1997.

Pert, Candace, Ph.D., *Molecules of Emotion*. New York: Charles Scribner's Sons, 1997.

Schulz, Mona Lisa, M.D., Ph.D., *Awakening Intuition*. New York: Harmony Books, 1998.

Shealy, C. Norman, and Caroline M. Myss. *The Creation of Health*. Walpole, N.H.: Stillpoint Publishing, 1993.

TAPES

Myss, Caroline, ENERGY ANATOMY: The Source of Personal Power, Spirituality & Health. Sounds True, 1996.

Myss, Caroline, THE ENERGETICS OF HEALING. Sounds True. Tel: (800) 254-8464. $49.98

Myss, Caroline, WHY PEOPLE DON'T HEAL. Sounds True. Tel: (800) 254-8464. $25.00

23

Mind/Body Medicine

What and When

Mind/Body Medicine combines Western medical practices with alternative health-care Bodywork techniques. It is focused on bolstering your body's natural healing systems by coordinating mental health and physical health. Many different techniques at the discretion of the doctor are used. This is medicine for those who think the body and mind must be healed together. Meditation is a key technique in this process.

Emmett E. Miller, M.D., has had a major role in the creation of the field of Mind/Body Medicine. His book, *Deep Healing,* presents his thirty years of experience in teaching self-healing. Dr. Miller believes that as our inner healing spirit is battered by trauma and neglect, it recedes from our consciousness, and we are deprived of its wisdom. Physical and mental diseases result from the alienation of this inner healing voice. Dr. Miller uses a variety of techniques to help us awaken our inner healers, including his own acclaimed guided-imagery tapes.

Jon Kabat-Zinn, a pioneer in Mind/Body healing, views mindfulness as the

At our essence is a divine "Knower," an inner healer and guide.

—EMMETT E. MILLER, M.D.

potential foundation for a new, highly cost-effective model of comprehensive health care in clinical medicine, medical education, and health promotion. The cardinal principle in doing this work is that it must come out of one's own extensive personal experience with meditation practice.

Jon Kabat-Zinn is codirector of the nationally acclaimed Stress Reduction Clinic at the University of Massachusetts Medical Center. In the Mind/Body program, which has been in operation for nineteen years, he and his colleagues have served more than ten thousand people with a range of conditions including heart disease, cancer, AIDS, chronic pain, stress-related gastrointestinal problems, headaches, high blood pressure, sleep disorders, anxiety, and panic.

The clinic was featured in a Bill Moyers PBS Special, *Healing and the Mind.* The primary work of the clinic is intensive training in mindfulness meditation. Research has shown that most participants in this training experience long-lasting physical and psychological symptom reduction, as well as deep positive changes in attitude, behavior, and perception of self, others, and the world.

Exercise

MIND/BODY STRESS REDUCTION: MEDITATION

Mind/Body Stress Reduction focuses on meditation training as the key to healing. There are many different meditation systems and techniques. The common core of meditation is the use of repetition of a physical act (counting breaths, reciting holy words, touching Mind/Body Medicine prayer beads, looking at

I started out thinking it was a bunch of hooey, but I've become a believer.

—C. GILLON WARD, MEDICAL DIRECTOR, JACKSON MEMORIAL BURN CENTER

symbols, walking rhythmically) to clear your mind of superficial thoughts and to
focus and calm you.

SITTING

+ Sit with your legs crossed loosely and your hands resting on your knees.
  Place a firm, slim pillow under your tailbone to allow your torso the slight
  lift forward that it needs to straighten, rather than curve backward. When
  you have found the appropriate angle, you can sit without holding your
  muscles. The alignment of the spine's vertebral column will support you
  without effort. You can relax more deeply.

+ If you prefer kneeling, you can place a pillow between your hips and calves
  for a similar lift. A small, rolled hand towel placed under your anklebones
  adds comfort by allowing your feet more cushioning.

CHIN POSE

Rest the back of each wrist on your knee as you sit in a meditation posture. Press the tip of your index finger against the tip of your thumb. The loop formed is meant to keep the vital energy within your body.

COUNTING BREATHS

+ With your spine erect, sit in a comfortable position with your knees bent, legs crossed. Close your eyes. Place your hands palms-up on your knees. Relax your breathing so you feel muscle movement low in your abdomen rather than high in your chest.

+ Begin counting your breaths. An inhalation plus exhalation is one cycle; the next inhalation and exhalation is number two, and so on. Try to hold this focus without being sidetracked by other thoughts or losing count until you reach number ten. It's harder than it sounds.

+ At ten, start again with one and count another ten breaths. Continue this cycle for a minimum of ten minutes. Gradually work up to longer sessions.

+ A clearing out of extraneous mental static is going on as you count and concentrate. You might imagine the thoughts moving across a film screen, passing into and out of view. Do not linger with the thoughts. Just notice them. Let them pass, and return to counting your breaths. Gradually, the thoughts will be spaced farther apart. The periods of neutral focus will grow longer. Don't judge the content. We all have countless ways to distract ourselves from our deeper purpose.

+ When you are in a relaxed, meditative state, you can try visualizing any body part that is sore, sick, or strained and see it as well and in perfect condition in order to encourage healing. Studies have shown that cancer patients and others recover more quickly when they employ meditative visualization than when they don't.

Spiritual Soundtracks

God respects me when I work, but He loves me when I sing.
—Rabindranath Tagore

A mantra is a mind song to soothe the savage body. A mantra can be one of the names of God, or simply a symbolic syllable, which is repeated in thought, or a sound to stimulate spiritual awakening. Sounds with different pitches have frequencies that resonate in different parts of the body. Sounds can be combined to reach the areas of your choice. Play yourself like a harp.

Om Chant

The Vedanta Sutra text from India, composed around the fifth century B.C., defines reality as that which persists in all circumstances. Most of the time we are caught up in changing ideas and pursuits. But now and then we see through surface illusions and have insight into more lasting perspectives. Yoga divides our average, muddled mindsets into three categories—waking, dreaming, and unconscious—all of which present distorted views of reality. Reality in yoga is the perspective beyond our personal viewpoint when we feel unity with the divine and see everything as part of this whole spirit.

The Aum Chant is an exercise designed to trigger this universal perspective through the repetition of sacred symbolic sounds of three Sanskrit letters. OM is the phonetic English spelling of the chant.

AUM is the Sanskrit word whose letters stand for:
A: the self in this material world,
U: the dream or psychic realm,
M: the unknown conscious.

Chanting these letters together in the sound of AUM can help unite our perceptions so that we experience a sense of our place in the larger cosmic order. The chant takes time to peel away the many layers of our illusions of separateness. Why not start today?

—Anne Kent Rush,
The Modern Book of Yoga

BOOKS

Bennett, Hal, and Mike Samuels. *The Well Body Book.* Random House, New York, 1973.

Chopra, Deepak. *Ageless Body, Timeless Mind: The Quantum Alternative to Growing Old.* New York: Harmony Books, 1993.

———.*Quantum Healing: Exploring the Frontiers of Mind/Body Medicine.* New York: Bantam Books, 1990.

Goldstein, Joseph. *The Experience of Insight.* Boston: Shambhala, 1993.

Goleman, Daniel, Ph.D., and Joel Gurin, eds. *Mind Body Medicine: How to Use Your Mind for Better Health.* Yonkers, N.Y.: Consumer Report Books, 1993.

Hanh, Thich Nhat. *The Miracle of Mindfulness.* Boston: Beacon Press, 1992.

Kabat-Zinn, Jon. *Full Catastrophe Living: Using the Wisdom of Your Body and Mind to Face Stress, Pain, and Illness.* New York: Delta, 1990, pp. 8–9.

Liberman, Jacob. *Light: Medicine of the Future.* Sante Fe: Bear & Co., 1991

Locke, Steven, M.D., and Douglas Colligan. *The Healer Within: The New Medicine of Mind and Body.* New York: E. P. Dutton, 1986.

Moyers, Bill. *Healing and the Mind.* New York: Doubleday, 1993.

Navarro, Vicente. *Medicine Under Capitalism.* Canton, Mass.: Prodist Publications, 1976.

Siegel, Bernie S. *Love, Medicine, and Miracles.* New York: HarperCollins, 1991.

Todd, Mabel E. *The Thinking Body.* Brooklyn, N.Y.: Dance Horizons, Inc., 1979.

Weil, Andrew. *Health and Healing: Understanding Conventional and Alternative Medicine.* Boston: Houghton Mifflin, 1983.

PUBLICATIONS

Integrative Medicine Quarterly Journal. For physicians and other health-care professionals. The first peer-reviewed scientific journal honoring this emerging field. Neither rejects conventional medicine nor embraces alternative medicine uncritically. Will publish original studies, review articles, major scientific reports, and debates on various health-care practices.

AUDIOTAPES

The Present Moment. Boulder: Sounds True (800) 333-9185.

Guided Sitting Meditation. Stress Reduction Tapes, PO Box 847, Lexington, MA 02173.

ORGANIZATIONS

Alliance/Foundation for Alternative Medicine
160 NW Widmer Place
Albany, OR 97321

American Academy of Anti-Aging Medicine
2415 N. Greenview Avenue
Chicago, IL 60614

American College for Advancement in Medicine (ACAM)
PO Box 3427
Laguna Hills, CA 92654

American Holistic Medical Association
4101 Lake Boone Trail
Suite 201
Raleigh, NC 27607

American Preventive Medical Association
459 Walker Road
Great Falls, VA 22091

Association of Natural Medicine
1 Espalda Court
San Rafael, CA 94901

British Holistic Medical Association
179 Gloucester Place
London NWI 6DX

Canadian Holistic Medical Association
491 Eglinton Avenue West
407 Toronto
Ontario M5N IA8

Center for Science in the Public Interest
1875 Connecticut Avenue, NW, Suite 300
Washington, DC 20009

Mind/Body Health Sciences, Inc.
393 Dixon Road
Boulder, CO 80302

Mind/Body Medical Institute
Division of Behavioral Medicine
New England Deaconess Hospital
One Deaconess Road
Boston, MA 02215
Physician's Committee for Responsible Medicine
PO Box 6322
Washington, DC 20015

VIDEOS/CDs

Adagio: Music for Relaxation CD	$15.00	
The Mozart Effect CD	Tel: (800) 254-8464	$39.98
The Mozart Effect Book		$23.98
Sound Body CD		$24.98
Yoga Journal's Yoga Remedies for Natural Healing	Tel: (800) 254-8464	$15.00

WEB SITES

Alternative Medicine
www-hsl.mcmaster.ca/tomflem/altmed.htm

Ask Dr. Weil

www.drweil.com

Andrew Weil, M.D., answers a new question each day on topics as varied as prostate cancer, love hormones, and smoking cessation.

Between the Lines

members.aol.com/pbchowka

Thoughtful analysis of the politics of alternative medicine.

Elsevier

www.elsevier.com/locate/intmed

Or call to subscribe at (888) 437–4636. Quarterly: $48/year for individuals, $98/year for institutions.

FeMiNa: Health and Wellness

www.femina.com/femina/healthandwellness

One of the largest resources on the Internet for women's issues.

General Complementary Medicine References

www.forthrt.com/-chronicl/archiv.him

Resources on topics from Ayurvedic medicine to Zen meditation.

HealthGate

www.healthgate.com

Source for health, wellness, and biomedical information.

Health World Online

www.healthy.net

Homeopathy Home Page

www.dungeon.com/-cam/homeeo.html

Homeopathy resources providing numerous links to companies that manufacture homeopathic remedies.

Med Web: Alternative Medicine

www.Gen.Emory.edu/med-web/medweb.almed.html

OncoLink, The University of Pennsylvania Cancer Center Resource

www.oncolink.org

Pages on cancer causes, screening and prevention, clinical trials of new treatments, financial issues for patients, and coping with grief and loss.

Southwest School of Botanical Medicine

chili.rt66.com/hrbmoore

Information on medicinal plants.

Yahoo Health: Alternative Medicine
www.yahoo.com/Health/Alternative_Medicine

Yahoo! Health: Women's Health
www.yahoo.com/health/women_s_health
Links women to an abundance of resources dealing with AIDS/HIV, birth and pregnancy, breast cancer, reproductive health, and more.

24.

Polarity Therapy

What and When

Based largely on Hindu Ayurvedic medicine, Polarity Therapy is a system of finger stimulation of two body pressure points at once in order to intensify the flow of electromagnetic energy through the body to speed healing. You can be clothed or nude and are usually lying down on a massage table. The sensations should not be painful, although they may feel intense if you experience increased energy flow in your muscles. Try it if you need a general energy renewal or if you have specific areas of discomfort.

Making Opposite Ends Meet

Learning to juggle might be good preparation for practicing Polarity Therapy. To do it well you need to be adept at working on at least two body points at once. Polarity Therapy is a complex system of healing that includes many different techniques, but the basics of some of the strokes can be used by the novice to wonderful effect for stress reduction and pain release. Dr. Randolph Stone, a chiropractor who spent years in India as a physician to a yogi, developed Polarity by combining his knowledge of Western Chiropractic manipulation with Eastern understanding of electromagnetic energy pathways in the body. Polarity techniques include massage, breathing, movement, and pressure-point stimulation.

Dr. Stone has written several texts outlining his techniques. In the early 1970s Dr. Stone returned to his native Chicago to train practitioners in the U.S. The American Polarity Therapy Association was formed in 1984 to certify practitioners and to help research, network, and maintenance of quality of practice.

A Current Treatment

Truly East/West Bodywork, Polarity is a combination of Indian Ayurvedic healing, Middle Eastern cabalistic teachings, Chinese Acupuncture, and Western Chiropractic manipulations. Polarity can be used to realign posture, release deep body and emotional tension, and treat particular medical problems. The word *polarity* refers to the use of two energy points simultaneously in order to balance the positive and negative electrical currents in the body.

- Polarity acknowledges a bipolar body life energy current that the therapist balances by using both hands to stimulate opposite trigger points. The right hand has a positive charge, the left a negative charge. The client's energy is rebalanced between them.

- Pressure should be applied extremely gently when you start. Only increase pressure on a point as the person you are touching relaxes and lets you know that more pressure is desired. As the person relaxes, very deep pressure on a point can feel wonderful and relaxing both to the point touched and to other areas of the body. No oil is used.

- The practitioner stimulates energy points on the client's body with the thumbs or fingers. Some Chiropractic manipulations are included. If the area stimulated is relaxed and in good health, the sensation there is not painful and often initiates waves of pleasurable feelings in the client's body, which move to different areas and relax the person even more.

+ If there is some kind of blocked tension around the pressure point and the tissue is contracted (hard or lumpy), pressure will be painful on that point. The discomfort will gradually fade away and become a neutral or pleasurable feeling as the energy released from the energy point spreads out and the client relaxes.

+ After a Polarity treatment the client usually feels refreshed, calm, and more alive. Over a period of time, along with the body and postural changes come parallel rejuvenating emotional changes. You can become more sensitive, energetic, and balanced.

Exercise

POLARITY THERAPY BACK AND SHOULDER POINTS

For learning relaxation of muscle tension in the back, shoulders, and legs, start by doing the pressure points on separate areas. When you feel comfortable with work on one area, you can try combining several pressure points at once. Like playing the piano, using both hands in different areas to stimulate several points takes a bit of practice, but the results are well worth the effort in relaxation and pleasure.

Exercise

WORKING ON YOURSELF

+ You can learn to apply pressure to hard-to-reach areas of your back by positioning yourself comfortably on your back on the floor or on a firm bed. Bend your knees and draw them up over your chest until you feel they can balance and rest there.

- Now make fists with both hands and slide them under your lower back so that your knuckles are pointing up and into the bony flat area of your sacrum. Allow the weight of your hips and lower back to press down on your knuckles.

- Close your eyes and allow your shoulders to relax. The weight of your back will sink more onto your hands. Keeping in mind the lower back, move your knuckles to other areas of your back as you feel one area relax.

TIPS FOR WORKING ON A FRIEND

- If you are working on someone else, pressure will be much easier to apply than on yourself. When your partner is resting on a mat on the floor, kneel beside her left hip so that you can easily reach the lower back.

- Working on a friend as she rests on a massage table or on a high, firm bed is often more comfortable for your back. Try not to strain your back as you relax your partner's.

- Stand beside your friend's hips to her left. Lean your weight onto your arms as you press your thumbs on either side of the highest sacral vertebrae. (Note the position in the illustration on page 193.) Gradually angle more of your weight down your arms into your hands, as you feel the person relaxing the muscle under your thumbs, or when she tells you to increase pressure.

- When you want to release pressure, do it as gradually as you applied it. If the release is sudden, it startles the person and undoes all the relaxation you've just induced.

- Now move your thumbs down to either side of the next sacral vertebrae.

- Apply the pressure of your body down your arms and into your hands resting on the back. Work in this way gradually from the top of the sacrum to the tip. Stay to either side of the vertebrae on muscle tissue. Most people have room for about three pressure points down the small sacrum.

- It is also relaxing to apply this same kind of finger or thumb pressure on either side of the outer edges of the sacrum. Define the arrow-shaped bone with your fingers. Work from just below the waist to the tailbone.

- The pressure should be deep but not painful. If it is painful, you are pressing either too quickly or too hard for your partner to relax. Or you might not be in quite the right spot, so shift your position and try another spot until your partner tells you it is comfortable. Done well, this feels good, even great!

Exercise

POLARITY THERAPY SHOULDER POINTS

- Sit or stand behind the top of your friend's head. Rest one palm lightly on each shoulder.

- Begin on either side of the neck. Using your thumbs, feel for the mound of the trapezius muscle that begins on either side of the neck and stretches out to the tip of the shoulder.

- Lean your body weight forward and down onto your thumbs so that you can gradually apply more pressure to the muscle. Hold the pressure in one place for thirty seconds or several minutes, whichever feels good to your partner (and to your thumbs).

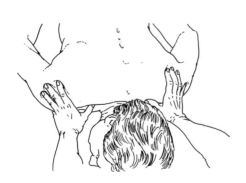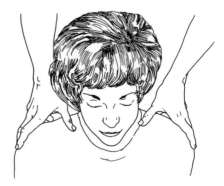

- If you find a spot along the trapezius muscle that feels tight, linger there a bit longer to give it time to release.

- Release pressure as gradually as you apply it. Make your way slowly from either side of the neck to the tips of the shoulders, holding pressure on each muscle area as you go.

Exercise

PUTTING IT ALL TOGETHER

Combining Shoulder and Lower-Back Points
for a Full Polarity Experience

- In Polarity Therapy a powerful relaxation of back tension can be achieved by pressing on shoulder and lower-back points together. You press on opposite shoulder and lower-back points when using them together.

- Imagine a large X on the back stretching from shoulder to hip. This defines your point pattern. When you press on the right shoulder, combine it with a pressure point on the left side of the lower back. As you apply pressure to points on the left shoulder, combine these with points on the right side of the lower back.

- Stand at your partner's left side so that your right hand is at your friend's lower back and your left hand rests on your friend's shoulders.

- In Polarity the right hand is thought to have a positive charge; the left hand has a negative charge. The healthful direction for the energy work you are doing is to move from the lower back up the spine to the shoulders and head. Positive energy will propel relaxing electromagnetic energy up the spine toward your left hand, whose negative energy attracts it. And this will encourage circulation to move toward the heart.

- Visualizing the large X pattern on your partner's back, press your left thumb onto a comfortable spot on top of the large trapezius muscle just to the side of the neck on your partner's left shoulder.

- Now press your right thumb onto a comfortable spot at the top of the right side of your partner's sacrum.

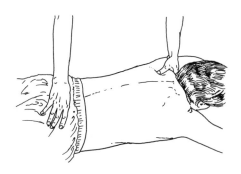

- Apply downward pressure on these opposite points simultaneously. Hold in place a minute or two. Tune in to any sensation you, or your partner, may feel moving between your two hands.

- Release very gradually.

- Now switch hand sides and press on the right shoulder with your left thumb, at the same time that you press on the left lower back with the right thumb. Hold a while.

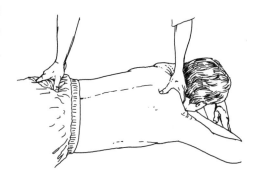

- Release gradually.

- You can work several points of the shoulder in combination with several descending points on the sacrum.

Exercise

POLARITY THERAPY SPINE POINTS

- Place your thumbs on either side of the top of the spine at the shoulders. Stay on the long muscles that run to either side of the spine. Do not press on the bones of the spine itself.

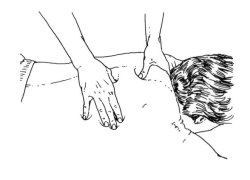

- Lean your body weight firmly and gradually down onto your hands. Angle your finger pressure slightly in toward the space between two vertebrae.

- Slowly release the pressure after a minute or so. Then move down the back to find the next lower notch between two vertebrae where you can apply your next finger pressure.

- Work methodically in this manner all the way from the shoulders to the tailbone. Take care you don't skip a vertebra or your friend will feel unfinished.

- When you reach the waist area just below the ribs, angle your thumbs toward each other so that you do not press down on the spine on the unsupported vertebrae of this area.

- Resume your downward pressure as you work over the sacrum. Then you can place the thumb of your left hand at the vertebra at the top of the left shoulder. Stand with the person's head to your left. Place the thumb of your right hand at the base of the spine on the sacrum on your friend's right hip. Apply simultaneous pressure to the two spots. Release. Move your thumbs one vertebra toward each other. Press. Continue until your thumbs meet on either side of the spine in the midback. Switch sides of the spine with your thumbs and repeat the sequence.

Exercise

THE STONE SQUAT

There are Polarity exercises you can do on your own that are designed to keep the qi energy, the source of life and health in Eastern medicine, flowing freely in your body.

- Stand firmly with your feet placed wide apart. Bend your knees and squat as though you are sitting in an invisible chair with your back straight.

- Place your palms on your knees, and hunch your shoulders so that a good deal of your weight is now resting on your arms.

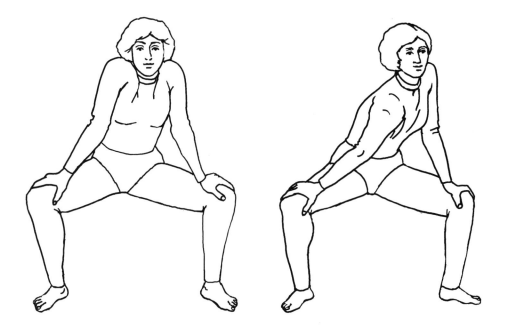

+ Then begin rocking from side to side, bending one knee while straightening the other. Your weight should be on your bent leg. Rock in place, keeping your foot on the floor.

Polarity Meditation Posture

+ Spread your legs apart and stand firmly on your feet. Bend your knees and slowly lower yourself into a squat position with your arms in between your legs and your feet as flat on the floor as is comfortable.

+ Then clasp your hands together. Spread your elbows and push outward against your knees.

+ Now relax your neck and head forward toward your hands. Close your eyes. Rest your head on your two thumbs, one thumb on either side of the bridge of the nose.

- Let your breath relax deep into your abdomen. You can rock a little back and forth (not from side to side) in this squat.

- A squat is like a sitting fetal position and helps release pressure on the lower back. It also lengthens the leg tendons and relaxes the shoulders. Placing your head on your hands in this position closes the body circuits by connecting your body extremities and creates a circular pathway for your electromagnetic body currents that is very soothing and energizing.

BOOKS

Chopra, Deepak, M.D. *Perfect Health: The Complete Mind/Body Guide.* New York: Crown, 1991.

Stone, Randolph, D.C., D.O., N.D. *Polarity Therapy: The Complete Collected Works on This Revolutionary Healing Art by the Originator of the System.* Sebastopol, Calif.: CRCS Publications, 1986.

Young, Phil. *The Art of Polarity Therapy: A Practitioner's Perspective.* Dorset, England: Prism Press, 1990.

ORGANIZATIONS

American Polarity Therapy Association
4101 Lake Boone Trail, Suite 201
Raleigh, NC 27607

British Polarity Council
Monomark House
27 Old Glouchester Street
London WC1N 3XX
UK

25.

Proskauer
Awareness

What and When

Proskauer Breath Therapy, or Proskauer Awareness, is a gentle system of posture-realignment and visualization training focused on small, light movements and slow, deep breathing exercises. You are fully clothed and lying down on a mat on the floor or on a bed. Try it after injury for realignment or for general stress reduction and imagery analysis.

The Pause That Refreshes

Proskauer Awareness is as gentle and relaxing as a sigh. Magdalene Proskauer, a graduate of the University of Munich, Germany, received a degree in physiotherapy from the University of Munich Medical School and headed the physiotherapy department of an orthopedic hospital in Munich. She worked in Yugoslavia at the Zagreb City Hospital, in New York at the Presbyterian Medical Center for the treatment of polio, cerebral paralysis, and posture corrections, and also in Los Angeles. Magda then settled in San Francisco, where she conducted classes in breath awareness and formed a private practice. Magda developed a precise and powerful therapy combining pause breathing awareness, movement release, and Jungian dream analysis. Her work is effective at a deep level because of its subtlety, gentleness, and focus on long-term rather than short-term psychological integration.

An Interview with Magda Proskauer

I work from the point of view that body and psyche are two aspects of the same reality, two manifestations of the whole personality that are in constant interaction. Our physical behavior seems to correspond to a psychic pattern of synchronicity. We mirror our psychological issues in our physical behavior. Synchronicity is a meaningful coincidence. For instance, if you study the dreams of people with back trouble you can find clues to the psychological correspondence with the back problem.

We can approach our problems both ways, physically and psychologically. The psychotherapist tries to bring the problem into consciousness through psychotherapy; the physical therapist works by approaching the body. Whenever we regress a little or fall back into an old pattern, the physical problems may come back again. And even if you know the psychological problem, you have to treat the physical. We have to learn to take care of our weaknesses.

I'm careful not to say, "This symptom goes with this psychological problem," because problems are pretty individual. Stomach ulcers are often connected with being overambitious. But it's dangerous to make absolute statements. All you can do is observe, when you work on the body, what the psychological problem might be. Most people who get these problems are not in their bodies enough. You help correct the problems some with more body awareness.

The person who has back trouble has to lie down before he or she gets a backache. After a long car or plane trip, even without having pain, they should lie down with the legs propped up, so that the back can rest, before it starts to hurt. Prevention is a tremendous education. Not everybody learns to live preventively, but when they learn, they're okay.

Visualization

People have to understand what is happening in their bodies to reap the most benefit from exercise. That is the reason I use visualization. Comparative medical studies show that patients who use visualization along with other treatments get better results than the patients who do not use visualization. I show my clients their X-rays. I make drawings of how the spine looks. If you can visualize it, you can feel it better. When you feel it, it works better than if you just do it mechanically. If you do it mechanically, you don't really release. You make mistakes.

You have to be aware and feel what you do in order for the exercise to work well. That's why the mechanical exercises, or those done too fast, contract muscles instead of release tension. It's also easy to strain again unless you are very subtle in your movements.

Visualization is encouraged by the particular kind of breathing that I teach. For instance, I ask you to breathe as if the breath were spreading out in the pelvis. One exercise is to try to relax the hip joint. When we are tense we pull our legs too far into the hip joint. You start by contracting and releasing the buttock muscles. I describe the hip joints to you as you move. I tell you the hip joint is made of a ball and socket. The socket part is created by the pelvis. The ball is the top of the thighbone. When we can release our tension the leg can come slightly out of the joint, and we create a little space between the socket and the ball. I talk anatomy to help you visualize it exactly. By visualizing this while moving, it can actually happen that the hip joint loosens up.

Body Talk

Then I say, "Feel the hip while you exhale." Some people can feel the hip joints. Then I make a shortcut and I say, "Exhale into the hip joints." This is impossible, but it's a helpful image. It really *feels* as if you can send your breath into the hip joints. I talk to the body directly.

I also give instructions to pause after the exhalation until the direct inhalation happens by itself. This helps to find our genuine rhythm. We breathe unconsciously or automatically from the moment we are born. We can also breathe consciously; we can stop breathing for a while and change our breath at will. The breath is like a bridge between the unconscious and conscious nervous systems. When you focus on the breath, you make a normally unconscious function conscious.

You can use your breathing to help make other unconscious functions more conscious. By focusing on the breath you may get in touch with certain unconscious emotions, for instance. That's why people sometimes cry when they start to relax from deep breathing. Dreams are an unconscious product, but if you remember the dream when you wake up, you bring this unconscious message into consciousness. Then you can learn to understand what it wants to tell you.

Some people even have visions during my exercise classes; some people don't. Jung encouraged people in what he called "active imagination," which is to concentrate in order to find one's images, but there are people who can't. Others can learn active imagination. Some people dream but can't remember their dreams. They are cut off from the unconscious. It's a very natural state to be in touch with your unconscious, but in our society there are many people that don't have visions or dreams. Some people can renew their contact with the unconscious by doing special breathing exercises.

—From *Getting Clear*
by Anne Kent Rush

Exercise

THE PROSKAUER PAUSE BREATH

There are different Proskauer exercises for each part of the body, but the same three-part breath is used in all of them. This breathing cycle is designed to trigger your own natural rhythm. By using this cycle you can let go of imposed rhythms (from speedy outside influences) and allow your own to surface.

+ Lie on your back on the floor. Relax your arms at your sides and let your feet fall outward. Close your eyes and feel the way you are lying on the floor. Notice whether any part of your body feels a bit tense or doesn't seem to be resting comfortably on the floor. Now shift your focus inside your body. Notice where you feel movement as you breathe.

+ If you feel tense anywhere, try imagining that you can breathe into the tension, as though you could actually exhale through that body part. Imagine the breath relaxing your sore muscle as it moves through it. *Breathing into a body part* is something you can do anywhere, anytime you feel tense or nervous. Locate the tight place and "breathe into it." The process is remarkably relaxing and can change the whole quality of your movement. Breathe in sync with the tensing (inhale) and relaxing (exhale) of your movement.

+ As you are doing this exercise, loosen your clothing if it is tight at the waist. Let the muscles of your stomach and abdomen relax and let your breath sink lower in your body. Place your hand palm-down at the lowest place on your torso where you can feel the motion of your breathing. Let your hand rest on this place awhile, until you begin to feel the rise and fall of your body under your palm from your breathing. Now let your hand and arm relax at your side again. If you see any pictures of yourself or other images during the breathing exercise, remember them and draw or write them down later.

+ Relax your jaw and open your mouth a little so that you can exhale through your mouth. You don't need to breathe heavily. Relax and breathe naturally. Inhale through your nose; exhale through your mouth; and pause at the end of the exhalation before you breathe in again.

+ This pause is the key to the effectiveness of the breathing. Crucial things are happening to your body during the pause; you are still actually exhaling, though you may feel that nothing is going on. Deepening your exhalation gets all the stale air out of your lungs, and makes more room for fresh air when you inhale. Most of us don't exhale deeply enough. Often, when you feel that you can't take in enough air, and that you'd like to inhale more deeply, it's because you haven't exhaled fully enough to make room in your lungs for new air. This is usually the breathing difficulty in asthma. Lengthening your exhalation can help release asthmatic symptoms.

+ You have paused at the end of the exhalation for a long time now. Let yourself really explore the pause. How does it feel to you? Does it feel too long? Not long enough? Are you a little worried that your body won't breathe in again unless you make it? Think of breathing when you are asleep. You don't have to tell yourself to breathe then. Think of animals breathing when they are resting. Their breath is long and rolling. They don't tell themselves to breathe. You can learn to trust that your breath will always come in again.

- Allow the pause to be as it wants. It may feel very long. See whether you can wait and stay with the pause until your body wants to breathe in again by itself. Inhale through your nose; exhale through your mouth; then pause and wait. It's a little like standing on the beach and waiting for another wave to come in. Try to find a pace at which you are neither forcing the pause nor making yourself breathe. Let yourself breathe in this pattern as long as you want.

- This exercise in itself is deeply relaxing. If you have difficulty going to sleep, you can use this breath at night. Or anytime you feel tense you can take a few minutes off for yourself, relax, and find your center again. It is a gentle, powerful centering exercise.

Exercise

IMAGE AND BODY MOVEMENT: PROSKAUER EXERCISES

Lower-Back Alignment

If we can visualize a body part, then we can usually feel it better. In order to keep in balance and to become more sensitive to our body's functioning, we can visualize our body parts as we move. We can also use other kinds of imagery to develop a sensitivity to body areas that are normally out of sight, such as the back.

Magda Proskauer's system of movement alignment combines breath awareness and visualization. Basic to the visualization in these exercises are the ideas of "breathing into a body part" and of "imagining how your joints and muscles look from the inside" as you move. Many of Magda's exercises involve imagining that you can breathe into your pelvis and sacrum, because the nerves and muscles of the sacrum are a major point of release for tension all over the body, especially the back.

- To begin this exercise, lie down on your back on a rug or mat. Can you feel your sacrum against the floor? Does it define a particular shape on the floor? Place your palm on your pubic bone. This bone is opposite the sacrum. The pubic bone, pelvis, and sacrum make a kind of bone girdle to support your lower internal organs. What shape is this "room?"

+ Imagine as you inhale that the air moves down through your body into your pelvis, filling up this bowl or room at the base of your spine. As you exhale, imagine that you can send your breath out through your sacrum, into the floor. This exhaling may give you the sensation that with your breathing you are putting down roots into the ground.

+ Now bend your legs, and bring your knees up toward your chest. Does this change the shape of your sacrum on the floor? Let your lower-back muscles relax as you "exhale through your sacrum." Allow the area to become as soft and comfortable as a pillow.

+ Now place your feet on the floor and press down, raising your sacrum slightly off the ground as you do. Take a small, air-filled rubber ball (about six inches in diameter) and place it under your sacrum in a comfortable place. Draw your knees up toward your chest again and find a place of balance for your legs. Let your lower back respond to the change of position that results from lying on the ball. Let your shoulders relax on the floor, and hang away from your ears. Allow your hips to relax and hang suspended on the ball. Continue breathing into the space between the pubic bone and sacrum.

+ Now imagine you can exhale through your sacrum into the ball and down into the floor. Continue this cycle for several minutes.

+ Now lower your feet to the floor, raise your pelvis slightly, and remove the ball. Gently lower your back to the ground, placing your hips down last. Do you feel any change in the way that your lower back is resting on the floor? Does your sacrum seem to have a different shape? Does your body feel tilted on the ground? If so, which feels higher, your lower back or your head?

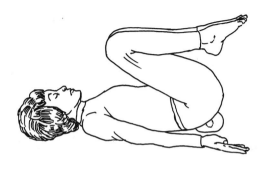

- Now sit up slowly, feeling the way your pelvis rests on the floor as you sit. Raise your body slightly off the ground with one hand, and place the ball under your tailbone with the other so you are sitting on the ball. Relax and find a comfortable position. Let your breath fill your pelvis as you inhale. As you exhale, imagine your breath flowing down your spine and through the ball into the floor. Do this several times.

- Then remove the ball and lower your pelvis to the floor. As you are sitting now, does the space between your "sit bones" feel any different on the floor? Do you feel a change in the angle of your back and the position of your spine over your pelvis?

Exercise

SPINE ALIGNMENT

If you have a healthy spine, this exercise helps you release tension in your back muscles and experience the relationship of the movement of your limbs to your spinal alignment. It should not be done by anyone with acute back pain.

- Kneel on the floor on a rug or mat. Lean forward. Touch your forehead to the ground, and relax your arms at your sides behind you, palms-up. As you inhale, raise your right shoulder up toward the ceiling slightly.

Imagine it is your breath that is doing the lifting. Feel your right shoulder blade move in toward your spine as it rises.

◆ As you lower your shoulder, imagine that you can exhale through a spot on your spine between your two shoulder blades. Use your breathing to keep your muscles relaxed and your movements smooth. As you exhale and lower your shoulder, let it fall toward the floor. Now try this lifting movement with your left shoulder. Shift the position of your head from time to time, even resting it to one side, to avoid getting a stiff neck.

◆ Next try the movement and breathing while raising both your shoulders simultaneously. As you lower them, release any tension in your upper-back muscles and see how wide you can let the area between your shoulder blades become.

◆ Roll over onto your side, and then onto your back on the floor. Rest awhile. Imagine that as you breathe you can exhale down the length of your spine. Imagine your breathing passing through the center of each vertebra as you exhale, relaxing all the nerves and muscles along your back.

◆ Lying on your back, take a rounded, straight stick (a dowel or debroomed broomstick will do) and place it under your spine. Lie down on the broomstick and see if you can relax your muscles enough to even out the pressure along your spine. The position should become comfortable. If you feel too much pressure on any point along your spine, "exhale" through that vertebra to relax the area.

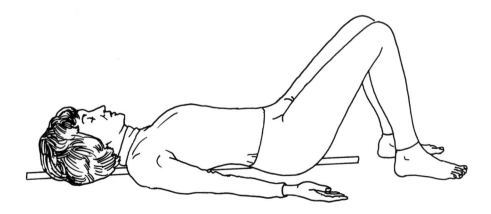

- After breathing comfortably in this position, take the stick out from under your back and lie down again. Notice any changes you might feel in the way your back is lying on the floor and in the way any parts of your body make contact with the ground.

- When you stand up after doing this exercise, experiment with movements of your arms and legs. Notice how the different movements of your limbs feel as though they originate from different sections of your spine. Try to keep this awareness as you move throughout the day.

Note on Research on Proskauer Awareness

Magdalene Proskauer wrote very little about her own work. Because of the power and importance of Proskauer Awareness in the Bodywork field, Anne Kent Rush, who trained with Proskauer for seven years in San Francisco, includes Proskauer interviews, quotes, and exercises in all her books on Bodywork.

26.

Subtle Energy Healing

What and When

Subtle Energy Healing is a system done by a practitioner in a meditative state, placing his hands gently on different parts of your body. This contact healing is often done during an operation or after one to relax the patient, but it can be used anytime.

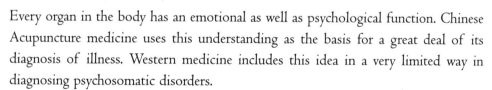

Every organ in the body has an emotional as well as psychological function. Chinese Acupuncture medicine uses this understanding as the basis for a great deal of its diagnosis of illness. Western medicine includes this idea in a very limited way in diagnosing psychosomatic disorders.

In his book *Subtle Energy: Awakening to the Unseen Forces in Our Lives,* William Collinge explains that intuition, meditative intention, and energy movement are forces that can be used to heal, transform, and lift us to higher states of creativity and insight.

Julie Motz became a Subtle Energy Healer in 1989. Her training includes Bioenergetics, Reflexology, Psychic Healing, Applied Kinesiology, Oriental Diagnosis, and Mind/Body Centering. Motz is a consultant for special projects to the Rosenthal

> What we call "personality" is not localized to the brain;
> it exists in every cell of every organ of the body.
>
> —JULIE MOTZ

Center for Alternative and Complementary Medicine at the College of Physicians and Surgeons at Columbia University. Motz teaches classes in understanding the anatomical and psychological characteristics of our organ systems as a tool for healing.

The body's four major organ systems are: the cardiovascular, the digestive, the respiratory, and the reproductive. Who we are is expressed in the development and functioning of each organ in our bodies.

Exercise

PALM SPHERE

This basic energy exercise can help awaken the world of healing in your hands. As you practice this exercise, its effects will become stronger so that you will feel intense energy and warmth in your palms and fingers. This energy can help relax the person on whom you are working. This training is basic to all touch-based healing systems.

+ Close your eyes. Sit comfortably. Rest your hands palms-up on your knees. Relax any tense muscles you feel by imagining that as you exhale, some tension leaves your body with your breath. Allow your breathing to sink low in your body so your belly puffs out a bit as you inhale and sinks back in as you exhale.

+ Now imagine what it would feel like if you could send your exhalation through the center of your body down your torso. Imagine your breathing can massage your muscles from the inside. Allow your breath to bring warmth and air to any tense areas. As you breathe, oxygen is drawn into your body and spreads through your bloodstream.

+ As you exhale, imagine you can send air down through your shoulders and arms.

I don't make a distinction between mind and body. What we call unconscious is all the information held in the body. Healing touch is a way of liberating that information and bringing it into the conscious. We have a habit, when we're in pain, of isolating that part from the whole body. The body has to listen to the information that part of the body has been holding from it.

I don't have to physically touch somebody. I ask them to tell me what was going on when the problems started, and as they talk, I scan their body, feeling in my own body where there is stress or blockage. When I feel stress in a body part, a strong emotion will come up under my hand. I'll explore that emotion with them as a way of liberating it.

—From an interview with Julie Motz

◆ You can even send warm air into your hands. What would it feel like if you could exhale down your arms and out the center of your palms through a spot about the size of a coin?

◆ Raise your palms so they are facing each other at about waist height. The increased circulation to your hands as a result of your breathing and visualization often brings a sense of warmth and tingling. The muscle relaxation and improved circulation allow the body's electromagnetic currents to move more easily. Can you feel any sense of this electrical flow between your facing palms? You can use this electromagnetic energy for healing.

- Some positions intensify the current. Allow your hands to move slowly in any direction they want. Try holding them different distances apart to see where the current feels stronger and where it weakens. You may sense a flexible shape to the airspace. Sometimes it feels as though you are holding a ball between your hands.

- The more you relax and direct your breathing down your arms, the stronger the sensation will become. This process releases tension in your shoulders and arms. You can use this directed breathing to relax tight muscles in other parts of your body.

- Healers learn to intensify this electromagnetic current so they can send relaxing sensations to other people. Being able to send and receive this energy gives you a resource for reviving tired muscles and spirits and for bolstering your healing powers.

BOOKS

Collinge, William. *Subtle Energy: Awakening to the Unseen Forces in Our Lives.* New York: Warner Books, 1998.

Motz, Julie. *Hands of Life.* New York: Bantam Books, 1998.

ORGANIZATIONS

International Society for the Study of
Subtle Energies and Energy Medicine (ISSSEEM)
356 Goldco Circle
Golden, CO 80401

Five

❖

Deepening

Your

Friendships

Introduction

How Can I Take My Bodywork Farther?

Advanced training and professional certification are available in all the systems. Sensory Awareness, meditation, and visualization techniques enhance the effects of the Bodywork and widen the scope of your abilities. These three systems are presented in this section because they are basic tools for deepening your body exploration. And happily, receiving more Bodywork is always vital to going farther.

> Except for sensations of pain and very general feelings of comfort
> or discomfort, the sensations from within are like the stars, which
> only appear when the artificial lights are turned off.
>
> —CHARLOTTE SELVER,
> *SENSORY AWARENESS*

How Is This Different from Bodywork Basics?

The basics of the techniques are exercises that anyone can do in a short amount of time. They give you a taste of a system in a simple way and are immediately useful. Advanced work in Sensory Awareness, meditation, and visualization require that you put aside some time each day to practice. The effects of the techniques strengthen when repeated over time. Gradually you learn to apply their benefits in more aspects of your life. You discover levels and layers to your exploration. You glimpse the fact that the exploration is endless.

Who Does What Where?

Contact the professional organizations that certify practitioners for referrals to reliable teachers and schools. Ask good practitioners where they studied. If you like their treatment, ask who trained them and try a treatment from their teacher.

Every Bodywork technique contains some forms of Meditation and Visualization. These practices improve your powers of focus and control. They also increase the power of all the basic exercises.

The Basics and Beyond

The systems presented in the previous chapters focus on your learning their techniques to reap their benefits. Sensory Awareness, meditation, and visualization are different in this area. They aim to free you from technique. Through very simple repetitive steps they take your body-awareness exploration beyond systems into deep states of relaxation and openness. These meditative states allow spontaneous insights to occur. Insight may come in the form of a feeling or a sound or a vision. If you practice the Sensory Awareness, meditation, and visualization steps consistently over time, you will become familiar with the meditative states they allow. You can learn to interpret the insights for your deeper mind/body awareness.

Keep exploring. You have at your fingertips a huge world to discover. There are many routes to take. Each technique offers a slightly different view of the landscape. Whether you take a short trip or a long journey, you'll find the basics of Bodywork useful and rewarding. The basic message you'll receive from your exploration into the realm of Bodywork is that the surprises, the powers, and the pleasures of the body are endless. Visualize healing. Visualize joy. How do they feel in your body?

Sensory Awareness

Charlotte Selver called her unique way of teaching us to deepen the authenticity of our experiences "Sensory Awareness." Philosopher Alan Watts, who often worked with her, dubbed Selver's work "living Zen" because it aims at understanding beyond intellectual learning. It is a kind of wide-awake meditation.

Charlotte Selver's Sensory Awareness is important because she was one of the original students of Elsa Gindler, "the mother of Bodywork," and because Sensory Awareness is Bodywork in one of its purest forms. There is no set course series, no anatomy or psychology training, no structural movements, no preconceived ideal of body image or motion, no guided imagery, no correct posture, no specific plan, no right or wrong. The teacher gives you guidelines for experiments to awaken your awareness of sensations during movement. These experiments help you sense yourself and others more clearly. You observe and allow more flexibility and honesty. With her partner, Charles Brooks, Charlotte, in her nineties, continues leading her extraordinary classes and influencing other teachers.

Exercise

FLY/WELCOME

+ Stand in a room, preferably with high ceilings and little furniture. Hold a rubber, air-filled ball. Choose one whose color, size, and weight feel good to you. Let yourself think about the ball and its pleasant qualities. Feel how this ball rests in your hands. Think of ways you might like to play with it.

+ Now toss the ball high in the air. As the ball leaves your hands, say, "Fly!" Follow its flight with your eyes. Can you let your feelings soar with the ball? Can you feel joy in its movement? How do your palms feel without the ball?

+ As the ball begins to move toward the floor again, prepare to receive it. Where do you need to stand to receive it easily? Feel its motion toward you.

+ As the ball comes into your hands, let yourself experience the return of its shape and weight. When it is in your hands say, "Welcome!"

+ Repeat this series ten times or so, experimenting with different moods of letting go and receiving.

+ Now try a variation with a partner, someone you like. Stand side by side. Your partner starts to run away very fast. As she leaves your side, say, "Fly!" How do you experience her leaving? How do you experience her flight? How do you experience yourself without her?

+ As your partner reaches the edge of the room, she turns and begins running toward you. How are you preparing to receive her? As she approaches, open your arms. When you meet, embrace and say, "Welcome!"

+ Repeat this sequence several times. Pay attention to your feelings about letting go and receiving.

+ Now trade roles so that your partner stands still, and you run.

✑   BOOKS   *✑*

Brooks, Charles. *Sensory Awareness: The Rediscovery of Experiencing Through Workshops with Charlotte Selver.* New York: Felix Morrow, 1986.

✑   ORGANIZATIONS   *✑*

Sensory Awareness Leaders' Guild
411 West Twenty-second Street
New York, NY 10011

Sensory Awareness Foundation
1314 Star Route
Muir Beach, CA 94965

28.

Visualization

What and When

Visualization is a healing system that uses imagery and guided meditation to help you create healthy conditions by imagining them. It can be used anytime.

Olympic Imagination

The value of visualization, long used in ancient systems of thought such as yoga, Shamanism, and witchcraft, is beginning to be recognized by some branches of modern medicine. One method frequently used in yoga is to see yourself doing a movement in your mind's eye before actually making the movement with your body. Such previsualization is a kind of practice that gives the effect of doing a movement twice. Athletes use visualization to increase their performance. Dr. Carl Simonton and his wife, Stephanie, in Texas are gaining renown for their successful treatment of cancers by encouraging their patients to use visual imagery of their bodies becoming healthy, along with other treatment, to stimulate their healing.

Visualization is a good form of healing for people who are too sick or injured to comfortably do exercises. It also can be a powerful addition to your physical routine, one that can help improve your image of your health. Visualization can be done at any time, even in situations where exercise may be impossible or inappropriate. You can make good use of time during those long car rides in rush hour or at dreary social events by imagining yourself going through the phases of your limbering exercises, soaring through the air as you ski-jump, or even being massaged to relax yourself.

Besides being a form of exercise practice, visualization can be used to encourage healing from injury, sickness, or imbalance. A simple and effective technique is to study anatomical drawings of the body part in need of healing. Then close your eyes, relax your breathing, and visualize that part of your body transforming itself into a healthy condition. As you develop the imagery, you may be surprised to find yourself imagining pictures of the body part undergoing changes, or seeing other kinds of imagery that give a symbolic message about the root of your problem or the pathway to improvement. Over a period of time you'll notice changes in the imagery, until you one day find your organ or body part mended. You can use this technique for prevention as well as healing.

Magdalene Proskauer, the San Francisco breath-awareness therapist, uses visualization as an integral part of her work. She encourages her students and clients to pay attention to the images in their dreams and waking visions, and to incorporate imagery into their body movements during her classes. Her Proskauer Awareness exercises often trigger visions that you can interpret on your own or with a therapist. Dreams and visions are messages from our unconscious and, therefore, doorways to normally inaccessible depths of our psyches.

If you can "see" a body part, you can feel it better. Once you have experienced the visualization exercises, such as Deep Fantasy, you may use the basic idea to invent your own exercises for any body part or condition.

Deep Thoughts

We all need to alternate periods of outward orientation and opening up to other people with phases of clearing these away in order to tune in to the inner life. Alternating this way keeps you balanced emotionally and nourished spiritually. You can tell you need to change when you feel either the need for more outside contact and fresh input, or when you feel overwhelmed and crowded by outside stimuli. When you have neglected your inner life you need to withdraw temporarily to be alone. Move back and forth between these two orientations not only over long time periods, but also within the space of each day for balance.

- ✦ Deep Fantasy and meditation are two different techniques that are useful for bringing you back in touch with your internal world.
- ✦ Deep Fantasy can be effective even when done sporadically.
- ✦ Meditation must be done regularly (each day, even just for a few minutes) to be fully experienced.
- ✦ Healing can be an aspect of both experiences.

Exercise

DEEP FANTASY

Deep Fantasy can be used for exploring your body internally for new "discoveries" or can be used as a healing process when you have a specific emotional or physical pain. Deep Fantasy is most easily done with an outside person acting as your guide, but you can learn to do it by yourself.

- ✦ The basic idea is to imagine that you can shrink yourself down into a tiny person; this tiny you can walk around until it decides where it wants to go, and then can enter your body to explore and perhaps do some internal maintenance. It is critical not to preplan a story; simply try to let the events occur. They will.
- ✦ Lie down in a quiet warm room on your back. Relax your breathing. If you have a specific ache or pain you want to work on, locate it and then choose the nearest natural body opening as your "entranceway." Imagine that you can shrink yourself to about a half-inch size or smaller. Talk out loud, and describe how this little person looks and is dressed.

- The journey in and out is just as important as the events at your destination. Try not to hurry or miss any steps. As you proceed, talk out loud explicitly about what you are doing and how it feels to you. If you have a pain in your shoulder you want to reach, you could enter through your mouth. Look around. Look at the settings and describe them. "I am walking up to the mouth. I am crawling over the lips. As I let myself down inside, the surface becomes slippery. It's dark in here. I'm walking toward the back of the mouth on the teeth. They feel sharp and bumpy. It's hard to get to my throat."

- When you reach the back of the mouth, you'll need to decide how to get down the throat (and later into the shoulder). "There's a deep hole here like a well. There's no way to get down except jump, but I don't know where I'll land." You can decide to go on or turn back and try another way. "I think I'll just jump." Describe your descent, what you see, how you feel. Almost always a surprise landing takes place; if not, pick something to catch on to to stop yourself or whatever, when you feel you've fallen far enough.

- When you land, decide how you're going to get to your sore shoulder muscle. You can swim through an artery or dig through a wall! When you reach the sore muscle, look around. Describe what you see. Try to figure out some way you could perhaps massage the muscle by walking on it or squeezing it. Imagine you are doing this and describe the process out loud as you go.

- When you are done, begin your journey out of the body any way you want. When you're out again, imagine you can blow yourself up to your normal size and merge with your large body again. Take a moment to check in to how the previously sore muscle feels now. Often it will feel greatly relaxed!

- One of the possibilities of this exercise is that some place or event may interest you on the way to your destination; if so, go with it. Perhaps you'll want to keep falling down your throat into your stomach to explore there. Or when you reach your sore muscle, you may find another person or animal "inhabiting" it. Talk to them and see if they "answer." Treat the fantasy the way you would a dream you were acting out and interpreting, in which each object and character is a symbolic aspect of yourself, offering to communicate. Use the fantasy journey to become more aware of your patterns. How do I deal with decision-making? How do I deal with fear and the unknown? How do I deal with obstacles? (Do I go around them, through them, or make a deal?)

This kind of visualization fantasy, though it may sound superficial, can actually be one of the most powerful techniques for opening up deep and usually unconscious body feelings. Practice it a few times on different parts of your body and with different aims (an old wound, an emotionally charged area) and sometimes without a specific destination, but simply to explore and go with what happens. You can also try doing this kind of internal fantasy exploration with a mate. What would it be like for you if your partner "came, too," imagining he was also journeying to massage your sore muscle and talking along with you? Pay attention to the dialogue between you and to what you can learn about your patterns by how you work out completing a task together.

Meditation

Meditation is another means of opening up to consciousness deep parts of yourself previously unexplored. While deep fantasy requires concentration on a specific vision, meditation requires you to let go of any visual pictures or any thoughts that may cross your mind. The easiest way to do this is to concentrate on your breathing.

+ Sit down, comfortably erect with a pillow under your sitting bones.

+ Stay focused on your breath rhythm and count up to ten (counting each inhalation and exhalation as one unit).

+ As thoughts come in, let them "pass through" instead of holding on to them. Let your attention be on your breathing.

+ After a while the mental static that usually jumbles us during the day will clear away, and the state of meditation takes place. This state is a pause between thoughts that can relax you and encourage mental and emotional perspective.

Many people think of meditation as a mental exercise. Ideally it is not; it is a way to open yourself to the deepest happenings in your body, and to allow these events to become part of your everyday consciousness. When you stick with it, just a few minutes each morning and a few minutes each evening changes the quality of your day.

There are many types and techniques of meditation to choose from. A fine book on the topic is *Zen Mind, Beginner's Mind* by Shunryo Suzuki. Another helpful book is *Concentration and Meditation* by Christmas Humphreys.

HEALING

Healing is not unusual or mysterious. A small cut on your arm will close and heal in a few days. Head-cold symptoms will heal in about a week. Many healings happen every day that we take for granted. Healing is quite ordinary; that is, everyone has healing powers. We either do not use them, do not know how to tap them, or don't label some of the things we do and feel as "healing" because it is not generally recognized in our culture as possible or even desirable.

Most healers consider regular meditation the way to mobilize the intuitive spirit in yourself and to open yourself to your unused inner powers. This is because the key to unblocking energy in someone else is being able to unblock your own. This is true of any of the "therapies" outlined in this book. The techniques can be learned by anyone; the depth and power with which they are used is dependent on the development and balance of the person transmitting them. What is most often therapeutic is contact with clear, centered individuals, along with ongoing development of your own awareness.

Meditation is one of the most powerful means to open your own channels to your deepest messages. It is also one of the most simple. Most healers prescribe a simple, daily, ten-minute-or-more meditation as the doorway to opening your healing powers. The meditation described earlier is fine. Tai Chi Chuan can be a moving meditation. And there are many more forms to choose.

Each person has a slightly different inner gift. This is what you are opening yourself to through meditation. For some people healing is their special form. For others the form can be teaching, writing, leadership, or spiritual development. The first stage is to get in touch with your individual power through a type of meditation. The second step is to learn to focus and direct your energy. The form you use may change as you change and as some other activity becomes more appropriate to your growth.

HEALING HANDS

The Palm Circuit exercise for Therapeutic Touch helps increase your healing abilities. This exercise gives you a chance to feel some of the sensations of channeling your energy in your body. Just as you could probably feel something (heat, vibration, magnetism, streaming, relaxation) in your arms and hands from this exercise, someone else could receive this energy into his body by making contact with you when you are relaxed, open, and focused. In a simple way this is the mobilization and exchange of healing energy. Physical and emotional tension block it. Relaxation, vitality, and centering increase it.

HANDS ON

+ You can channel healing energy throughout your body. It seems to be particularly strong through your arms and hands. To experiment, lightly rest your right hand (palm-down) on any spot on a friend's body that is tense or sore.

+ Place your left palm on any other part of his body. (One especially good position is to have your hands opposite each other—that is, your right hand, say, for stomach pain, on the stomach and your left hand opposite it on the back.)

+ Close your eyes and relax your body. Focus your attention on your breathing and begin "exhaling" out your palms.

+ You can also try imagining that the tension is moving from your right hand toward your left and dissipating.

◆ After five minutes or so, slowly take your hands away and ask your friend if any of the soreness or tension has gone.

SELF-HEALING

Meditation and centering are two basic forms of self-healing because they are means of rearranging unbalanced energy (unhealth) and balancing (health) the flow throughout your body. Another approach is to use images. If you have an ear infection or a liver problem, for example, you could find a picture of a healthy ear or liver in a medical book and spend ten minutes a day visualizing your ear or liver to look just like these healthy ones. You can also do this visual healing with someone else's ear or liver.

The idea is that the organ is "sick" because you have withdrawn the life energy from that part by tension. By focusing your attention on the neglected parts and allowing life energy, spirit, and joy to move through them again, you can heal.

BOOKS

Achterberg, Jeanne. *Imagery in Healing: Shamanism and Modern Medicine.* Boston: Shambhala, 1985.

Capra, Fritjof. *The Tao of Physics.* Boulder: Shambhala, 1975; New York: Bantam, 1977.

Cousins, Norman. *Anatomy of an Illness as Perceived by the Patient.* New York: Norton, 1979; New York: Bantam, 1981.

Epstein, Gerald. *Healing Visualizations: Creating Health Through Imagery.* New York: Bantam, 1989.

Samuels, Mike, and Nancy Samuels. *Seeing with the Mind's Eye.* New York: Random House, 1975.

Schucman, Helen. *A Course in Miracles.* Tiburon, Calif.: Foundation for Inner Peace, 1976.

Schwarz, Jack. *Voluntary Controls: Exercises for Creative Meditation and for Activating the Potential of the Chakras.* New York: Dutton, 1978.

Simonton, O. Carl, Stephanie Matthews-Simonton, and James Creighton. *Getting Well Again.* Los Angeles: J. P. Tarcher, 1978; New York: Bantam, 1980.

ORGANIZATIONS

Academy for Guided Imagery
PO Box 2070
Mill Valley, CA 94942

American Imagery Institute
4016 Third Avenue
San Diego, CA 92103

Center for Applied Psychophysiology
Menninger Clinic
PO Box 829
Topeka, KS 66601

Esalen Institute
Highway 1
Big Sur, CA 93920

International Imagery Association
PO Box 1046
Bronx, NY 10471

Omega Institute
260 Lake Drive
Rhinebeck, NY 12572

VIDEOS/CDs

The Four Noble Truths (video)	$109.00
(His Holiness the 14th Dalai Lama's basic tenets of Buddhist thought as seen on PBS—6 hours.)	
Health (video)	$20.00
Healing (CD w/booklet)	$25.00
(Healing Arts Catalog)	
Healing Words—Guided Imagery	
Weight Loss	$13.00
Headaches	$18.00
Smoking	$13.00
Multiple Sclerosis	$13.00

Lupus/Arthritis	$13.00
Chronic Pain	$13.00
Cancer	$13.00
Stress	$18.00
General Wellness	$13.00
Alcohol	$13.00
Heart Disease	$13.00
Depression	$13.00
(Healing Arts Catalog)	

Index

A